Multicultural
Counseling
Workbook

Exercises, Worksheets & Games
to Build Rapport with
Diverse Clients

Leslie E. Korn, PhD, MPH, LMHC

"In this invaluable handbook, Dr. Korn has thoughtfully brought together a much needed collection of effective exercises for engaging in discussions on a wide-range of equity-related topics. The text begins by laying a framework and then offers many creative ways to stimulate insight and reflection. It will be an essential companion for clinicians, therapists, teachers, educators, community activists, consultants and equity committees."

-Robin DiAngelo
Author of *What Does it Mean to Be White? Developing White Racial Literacy*

"Leslie Korn has produced an impressive, highly accessible workbook on diversity and rapport building that will be of great benefit to counselors and professional help givers. Most importantly, it provides invaluable tools and exercises to facilitate better recognition, understanding and processing of feelings and beliefs regarding diversity in those of us who work in counseling. It is at the same time comprehensive and learned, yet highly readable with many case examples and illustrations. It is a gift to those who wish to be more adept in practicing in a more diversity-sensitive manner."

-John Ludgate, PhD
Author, Psychologist, Fellow of the Academy of Cognitive Therapy

"A comprehensive, collaborative and insightful workbook, it offers the clinician opportunities to reflect on their personal cultural identity and socialization while encouraging a deeper understanding of the role of power, privilege, and the complexities of culture, ethnicity and race in other cultural communities. This workbook provides practical worksheets to help professionals moreover establish rapport and relationship with their clients. Dr. Korn's book is a gift to the field of mental health and will support culturally responsive professionals."

-Priscilla Sanville, PhD, Professor Emerita,
Creative Arts in Learning and Social Justice
Lesley University, Cambridge, MA

"A wise traditional birth attendant from Darfur once told that '*knowledge is like a garden: if it is not cultivated, it cannot be harvested.*' Leslie's workbook is an effective fertilizer to cultivate multicultural counselling in the garden of clinical knowledge. It's a great resource for clinicians and healers to develop multicultural competencies and mindfulness to diversify their work. It can also be used as a "refresher" for many kinds of helping professionals."

-Janaka Jayawickrama, PhD
Lecturer and Community Care Practitioner
University of York, United Kingdom

"*The Multicultural Counseling Workbook* provides an abundance of information about the cultural experiences of a variety or ethnic and other cultural groups, as well as practical exercises that encourage honest reflection, help identify assumptions and subconscious influences, while also challenging them to move beyond them. Some of the workbook's best moments are vignettes that show Dr. Korn's efforts to address sensitive topics, assess cultural influences and build therapeutic rapport with a variety of clients. I would recommend this workbook to mental health professionals seeking to increase their own as well as their client's cultural knowledge and self-awareness."

-Lambers Fisher MS, LMFT, MDIV
Approved Supervisor, Minnesota Board of Behavioral Health

"As a university faculty member and clinical practitioner, I think Dr. Korn's book is a wonderful, comprehensive and much needed resource for cultural competency development. The narrative assists the reader in the exploration of one's personal cultural self-awareness and helps the acquisition of new skills. I found this workbook to be the best multicultural counseling field guide I've read in many years. It provides a thorough compilation of information, worksheets and exercises that clinicians will value for a long time to come."

-Dinah Manns, EdD, Research Lead/
Faculty, Human Behavior-Counseling Studies
Capella University, Minneapolis, MN

"Dr. Korn's multicultural counseling workbook is challenging, innovative, thought-provoking, educative, and experiential. All the qualities you want in an engaging workbook. When families and nations struggle behind unconscious masks of prejudice and bias, all efforts to heal illusions are welcome. This book is a valuable tool for nurturing change."

-Joseph Randolph Bowers, PhD
Senior Counseling Psychotherapist: Cultural, Indigenous, Disability, and
Mental Health Specialist University of New England, Australia

"The importance of multicultural competency in our conflict-ridden world can't be overstated. It is in everyone's best interest. But the work involved in disentangling one's prejudices is intense, and this book is here to help. Designed for clinicians and clients and children as well as adults, there is something here for everyone. Teachers of undergraduate and graduate courses in social services are likely to find this book especially useful as they prepare students for work in the field. This is the kind of book that clinicians and graduates are not likely to resell because it will be useful on a day to day basis if they embrace the values involved."

-Estelle Disch, PhD
Professor Emerita of Sociology
University of Massachusetts, Boston

Published by
PESI Publishing & Media
PESI, Inc
3839 White Ave
Eau Claire, WI 54703

Cover: Amy Rubenzer
Editing: Marietta Whittlesey & Karsyn Morse
Layout: Bookmasters & Amy Rubenzer

ISBN: 9781559570404

Printed in the United States of America.

PESI
Publishing
& Media
www.pesipublishing.com

Contents

Epigraph

"The words for "people" are so beautiful that they sing. Listen as you say Inuit (IN uu EE), Naga (NAAg), Lakota, Hopi, Yanomami (YAA no MOMee), Ainu (EYE new), Mong, Palau (baa LOW), Karimojong, Dogon (DOE gone), Yup'ik, and Taidnapum (ti ID-NAA-pum). By these words and thousands more spoken in more than six thousand languages we immediately recognize the richness of human diversity joined by common knowledge."

— Rudolph C. Ryser, Ph.D.
Center for World Indigenous Studies

Acknowledgements

A book like this is always a collaborative project, enriched by the variety of people who contribute their ideas and suggestions through their cultural expertise and instructive exercise savvy. My former doctoral students, Dr. Keitha Wright contributed innovative exercises on resiliency, and Dr. Jeremy Northrop's work informed the section in Christian counseling. Dr. Robin DiAngelo graciously contributed a section on white fragility, based on her work as a diversity educator and Dr. Rose Lapomarel provided insight in Haitian cultural practices. My interns Julia Hankin, Esther Devannay, Ashley Barad, Valerie Nguyen and Haley Oberg, and my colleague Annie Ochoa all made important research and written contributions about various cultures and religions. I am indebted to the Center for World Indigenous Studies research associates; Dina Gilio Whitaker nimbly contributed to several sections on a variety of cultural identities and practices, and Heidi Bruce contributed to the sections on refugees and the Irish. My assistant Marlene Bremner provided skilled and focused editorial support for this fourth book of ours together. I am grateful to her for her commitment to this project.

I am forever grateful to the people of the Comunidad Indigena de Chacala, Mexico, with whom I have lived and worked for much of the past 40 years. I have learned much about myself and about the mental and physical well-being of diverse communities as a welcome guest in their towns and villages.

My husband and colleague, Dr. Rudolph Ryser, and I have been engaged in developing many of the concepts and exercises in this book over the last 20 years. His influence on my thinking is inestimable. He embodies a generosity of spirit and willingness to review and edit my writing, which inevitably results in a better book. I am ever so grateful for his wise counsel and "electronic" pen as well as the joy and humor he brings to our lives together.

Introduction

"Cultural competency begins with knowing who you are."

— Rudolph C Ryser, PhD,
Center for World Indigenous Studies

The United States population of more than 300 million includes individuals and groups from most of the world's 243 countries and peoples along with more than 550 indigenous nations. Engaging the diversity of one's country can be a challenge, but it can also be enriching while offering an expansive understanding of the world in which we live.

When we take a history or conduct an assessment, we are listening to someone's story and often asking them to make meaning of the story; through words or bodily symptoms. Understanding the diversity of stories across cultures illumines our capacity to understand more deeply the meaning of our client's stories. But in order to do so we must first understand our own varied stories. While we often explore our psychological story, our family story or our somatic stories, we do not quite as often in our clinical training explore the role of our cultural stories in contributing to our identity as individual clinicians, healers, colleagues, and administrators. This book provides a door to that path of exploration.

HOW TO USE THIS BOOK

This workbook is designed for use by mental health and physical health clinicians and therapists, who want to develop new skills, explore their own attitudes and prejudices that can get in the way of a fully engaged diverse clinical practice and to obtain information about other cultures, religions and gender/sexual orientation. Groups of practitioners who want to increase their skills, and apply new tools for themselves and their clients as part of group professional development may also find this book helpful. I have designed many of these exercises to be conducted while sharing a potluck meal to deepen self-knowledge and, to share in a safe space, feelings and attitudes that can also be a barrier to deeper collegial connection.

I have included many exercises and worksheets for you to use by yourself or with colleagues. There are also many worksheets, exercises and games you can use directly with clients to build rapport and connection. These exercises convey knowledge and they are fun. They draw on the many the ways we communicate through words, our body and through the arts and games. **For your convenience, you may download a PDF version of the handouts at go.pesi.com/multicultural**

To illustrate techniques and methods for establishing connection between the clinician and clients with different cultural experiences I have selected some of the larger and a few of the smaller cultural and religious identities present in the U.S. population. I have included cultural identities from all of the populated continents and some of the islands. You will learn about these cultural identities and by so doing you will further develop competencies to understand best practices that can be useful for you engaging cultural identities not emphasized here. I go into depth with some cultural identities such as Mexican, Native American, African American and Asian and emphasize less several other identities. The richness of cultures will become apparent to you as you enter into your own extended learning even as the exercises in this workbook give you practice. We will also explore religion, spirituality, gender, sexuality, and disabilities.

At the end of each chapter you will find a range of multimedia resources that will extend the concepts presented in the chapter. **These can also be accessed at www.healthalt.org**

WHY DO WE NEED THIS BOOK?

When I work with groups of clinicians around the United States I usually divide the world into, (1) Persons rooted in a culture and, (2) Those who have not been schooled in their own culture or who have simply set aside their culture to adopt another way of life. I frequently hear people say, "Oh, I don't know who I am, I'm just Heinz 57!" While each of us may not initially comment on culture and ethnic identity with people who say they are from one or more Euro-American heritages, there may be many reasons to step up and name one's heritage.

What might some of these reasons be? For one thing, naming one's heritage gives one a sense of grounding and connection with family, ancestors, and history. Understanding one's heritage also allows one to greet and understand other people and their family ties. Understanding one's personal cultural heritage sometimes has the interesting effect of explaining why a person prefers a particular climate, a place, and even why one prefers certain cuisines. Children taught to understand their cultural heritage are more ready to respect and understand the diversity in their social lives while learning from that diversity.

Knowing one's heritage provides an opportunity to expand one's own knowledge and appreciation of other cultures and to find a balance in life.

Chapter 1
Setting the Stage for Competency

Chapter 1
Setting the Stage for Competency

"Empathy is the most radical of human emotions."

— Gloria Steinem

CULTURAL COMPETENCY

Cultural competence is fundamental to our work. Although cultural competence with diverse populations historically referred to individuals and groups from non-northern European national origins, the idea has evolved to include differences pertaining to sexuality, religion, creeds, and physical and mental ability. While some of us may be lucky enough to travel to different places in the world where there is so much diversity along these lines, most of us will encounter the world's cultural differences in the United States and even in our own town or community. The United States has been a final immigrant stop for more than 200 years with people enriching our arts, music, technology, government and even our educational systems. Not only have people emigrated, but the original peoples of the Americas whose ancestors first began living in the country more than 14,000 years ago live in the American multi-cultural reality. After thinking about all of this, one might conclude that America is really a reflection of the world's many cultures where diversity persists to the enrichment of all.

Some social commentators suggest that the cultural competence model is largely ineffective. They go further to say that its tendency is to divide people into cultural camps or to equalize and normalize oppressions under a "multicultural umbrella." Others argue that the model unintentionally promotes a color-blind mentality that hides the significance of institutionalized racism.

Whether cultural competence recognizes the rich contributions and value of human cultural diversity or serves to divide people into camps or shields bigotry and racial discrimination it is a practical reality that cultural differences and human diversity exist and, as clinical practitioners, we are confronted with the reality in our everyday profession. Learning cultural competency opens one to the world of human diversity.

Cultural sensitivity is about your tolerance to:

- Age
- Color
- Culture
- Disability
- Ethnic identity

- Gender identity
- Different language(s)
- Religious practice, spirituality
- Sexual orientation
- Socio-economic status

Who are we? What defines us? How does what we say about ourselves change with different people and different situations? How can we deepen our sense of self and the multiple identities we express?

In order to know another person—another culture—we must first know ourselves: our own cultures and identities.

I have designed the exercises in this chapter to support your strengths and shore up your capabilities as a clinician. Your learning goal is to strengthen your personal cultural awareness and awareness of those around you.

WHO AM I?

Directions: Do this with a partner or with a few people. Each person takes 15 minutes to answer the following questions and form a narrative about their ancestry.

If you are doing this alone use the spaces below to write your thoughts.

Where do you and your peoples come from?

_____

_____

_____

_____

_____

What ancestors arrived before you to enable your birth and where did they come from?

_____

_____

_____

_____

_____

What family stories do you know about your heritages? What is hidden or secret?

_____

_____

_____

_____

_____

MINDFULNESS

Directions: Take 5 minutes to breathe, quiet the mind and check in personally about this process of self-exploration about identity. Allow your thoughts and feelings to rise to the surface. Let your thoughts and feelings rise into your awareness, observe what you find, and let then them fall away as you watch them transform. Let them continue to come in and let them drift out with each exhalation.

How do you feel exploring the topics identified in this workbook?

_____

_____

_____

_____

_____

_____

_____

Are some areas more comfortable for you than others?

_____

_____

_____

_____

_____

_____

_____

As you consider various exercises in this book, return to your breathing and moment-to-moment awareness to think about your thoughts and feelings as you do exercises alone, with a client, or with colleagues, family, and friends.

MIGRATION STORY

Traumatic experiences have affected every cultural group in the United States today. With the exception of peoples indigenous to the western hemisphere, people living in the U.S. migrated here at some point in their lives or their ancestry. The arrival of the Europeans had varied effects on the more than 500 tribes of indigenous peoples populating every corner of the continent. The effect on the lives of indigenous peoples on the continent was often traumatic. Before the 17th-century arrival of religious refugees escaping persecution in England, the Spaniards arrived in Mexico, Puerto Rico, and California. Between the 16th and 19th centuries, Chinese, Philippine, and African people arrived under traumatic conditions, often as slaves. These effects, on both mental and physical health continue to reverberate today.

 Most of us have a migration story, what is yours?

My Migration Story

I am the daughter of two assimilated Jews who experienced significant structural anti-Semitism (college quotas, hotels and club refusal) even as they grew up in the enclave of Jews who migrated from Eastern Europe to the east coast. Where I grew up in the suburbs of Boston it was customary to introduce ourselves with information about where we went to school, what our degrees were and what jobs we held.

When I went to live and work in rural Mexico, no one cared about where I went to school or what degrees I had, nor what jobs I had held. People were more concerned with who I was, and if I had the patience to sit with them for hours, or walk into the jungle. Or, they wanted to know if I was available at 11:00 pm for an appointment when they were already 8 hours late for their original time at the clinic. In short, they were concerned with if I was who I said I was: authentic and present.

One of the things I learned from my husband, whose mother was Cree and Anishinabe, and whose father was Swiss, and who was raised among the Quinault on the Pacific West Coast, is that when you introduce yourself you describe not only your name and where you live, but who your parents and grandparents and great grandparents are and where they lived.

MIGRATION STORY

Directions: Answer the following questions, either alone or with a partner.

What is your migration story? What types of migration trauma did your family experience? Were they fleeing oppression? Once they arrived where did they settle? Were they in an enclave of people from their country of origin or were they isolated? What did they experience in terms of exclusion?

_____

_____

_____

_____

_____

_____

_____

_____

What are/were the ritual/spiritual/religious practices of your ancestors?

_____

_____

_____

_____

_____

_____

_____

_____

_____

YOUR NAME, YOUR HERITAGE

Our names tell a lot about who we are and where we come from. In many societies a person's surname or family name may be derived from an ancestor's home region, or some quality of the land. As a result, surnames can sometimes lead one to know the land where early family members first acquired a name. Until only a few hundred years ago most people was given one name (first name) and that was all they were known by.

But, when the world and local population began to grow in the 1500s (when the population of the world was about 460 million or just a little larger than the U.S. population in 2014), and governments like the kingdoms of Europe, emirates of the Middle East and new countries like France and the United States began to impose taxes on individuals it simply wouldn't do to have three members of one family with the name John or four members with the name Mary. Last names became necessary. The son of John would become John Johnson. The daughter might take on a different name as a surname. Some names would derive from a location as in Ms. Riverton or a Mr. Rockton. The names may be now derived from a parent or grandfather or grandmother's name.

The consequence of the naming patterns over the last 500 years is that names now tell stories of families, lands, and times in history.

My Name is Leslie Ellen Korn

Leslie was a popular name given to girls in the 1950's. It's a suitably English name for Jews "passing" in America. Ellen is the Anglicized version of my Hebrew/Yiddish name Elka. (עלקא) It is a Jewish tradition to name a child after a deceased relative, hence my middle name. Finally my name Korn is my grandfather's name unchanged, as an immigrant from a long series of grain (korn) farmers in and around Silesia on the Austro-Polish border. While my father's family did not change their name (nor did I take my husband's name when we married) my mother's family's name Finberg was fraught with attracting anti-Semitic behavior leading some relatives to change the name to the more innocuous Finley.

One more note on my name. When I arrived in the jungle of Mexico, Leslie as a name was unknown and difficult to pronounce. So, people pronounced it "Lexi" which was short for Alex which is short for Alexandra. Hence I became known, and I am still called, Alexandra in Mexico.

YOUR NAME, YOUR HERITAGE

Directions: Answer the following questions, either alone or with a partner.

Do you know what your first, middle and last names mean or refer to?

_____

_____

_____

Where does your name come from?

_____

_____

_____

Why were you given these names?

_____

_____

_____

Have you ever thought of changing your name or have you changed your name? Why?

_____

_____

_____

Has anyone ever assumed you were a particular ethnicity because of your name? Were they correct? Partially correct? All wrong?

_____

_____

_____

Have you ever assumed someone was a particular ethnicity because of his or her name? Were you correct? Partially correct? All wrong?

_____

_____

_____

_____

How do you feel about each your names?

_____

_____

_____

If your family (ancestor) was originally from a country other than the U.S., (Europe. Africa, Asia, for example) did they change their name? Was it changed for them? If so, why? How do you react to that?

_____

_____

_____

_____

Think of a time you met someone with a last name that you assumed meant a certain heritage. Did you later discover that …

It was their married name?

It was a name of an ethnicity other than their own?

_____

_____

_____

_____

THE FAMILY CULTURE

The following exercise explores the concept of family culture and then draws upon early interfamily experience. Joe Hatcher developed this exercise to explore what he calls: "the first culture," and to illustrate how family norms can differ from family to family.

Ask your client to fill out the following Quick Family Culture Scale and use it as a jumping-off point to discuss ways in which these norms have persisted or ways in which the resulting behaviors may have been rejected or altered.

QUESTIONNAIRE
QUICK FAMILY CULTURE SCALE

Directions: Circle the alternative that best describes the norms of your family as you were growing up.

1. **How often did you eat your evening meals together as a family?**

   Always   Most of the time   Occasionally   Never

2. **How often did the members of your family hug to display affection?**

   Very often   Rather Frequently   On special occasions   Never

3. **How often did the members of your family express verbal affection for each other?**

   Very often   Rather Frequently   On special occasions   Never

4. **What were the rules for expressing disagreement in your family?**

   Blunt honesty   Direct, but courteous   Indirect   Not encouraged

5. **What were the rules for expressing anger in your family?**

   Yelling okay   Showing anger okay   Talking Okay   No anger shown

6. **Was your family "competitive" with each other, in terms of playing games, or using humor at the expense of others?**

   Always   Very often   Seldom   Never

7. **How important were sports in your family?**

   Extremely   Moderately   A little   Not at all

8. **The traditional sex roles in our society often involve men having a career and women taking care of children and the house. With that understanding, how traditional would you describe the sex roles of your family?**

   Very   Mostly   Non-traditional, i.e. equal   Counter-traditional

9. **What was the attitude of your parents toward your education?**

   Extremely supportive   Moderately supportive   A little supportive   Uninvolved

Reprinted with Permission Hatcher, J. W., Parks, M. W., & Suesser, K. (2013). *Using Family Culture to Illustrate the Basics of Intercultural Interaction: An Exercise to Teach the Problems and Potential of Cross-cultural Interaction.* Retrieved from http://www.uwosh.edu/hst/?p=499

COMMONALITIES AND DIFFERENCES

Directions: Work with a partner or small group.

Identify a few things you all have in common and one thing that is unique to each of you.

_____

_____

_____

_____

_____

_____

_____

_____

What did you discover about yourself as a result of this exercise?

_____

_____

_____

_____

_____

_____

_____

_____

_____

OUR MYTHIC STORY

Our clients tell us stories about their lives. We help them make sense of them and often help them transcend their mundane story into something that holds greater meaning, leading to purpose and a life plan. At a certain stage of recovery, when working with people who have been victimized it becomes time to "leap" over the victim story (not forget) but to forge a bridge to another place in one's life story in order to create a post victim life. One of the ways I do this with a client is to ask them to consider themselves as the hero of their own journey. We begin by identifying their favorite mythic hero and then write their own story in mythic terms.

There are many resources to support this if a client does not have a story in mind. It may be drawn from fairy tales, or specific cultural tales or Greek myths. When working with trauma survivors I may suggest the trauma stories of heroes like Persephone, Inanna or Achilles. Or it may be the story of the Mayan Hero Twins, Hunahpu and Xbalanque, or Oya, the Yoruba warrior-spirit of the wind, lightning, fertility, and fire.

OUR MYTHIC STORY

Directions: Think about an important mythic story. It may be the Greek story of Persephone and Demeter, Iananna, Hercules, stories of heraldry from the English. Or it can be just a great story of transformation. Tell your story as though you are this mythic person, perhaps a hero adventurer, crone, or mystical wise person.

_____

_____

_____

_____

_____

_____

_____

_____

_____

_____

_____

_____

_____

_____

_____

_____

_____

_____

ARE WE SHARING CULTURAL WAYS OR APPROPRIATING THEM?

Since the earliest days of contact between European and indigenous American cultures, many settlers and descendants of settlers have adopted the life ways of America's original peoples. From the very beginning of the colonial era Europeans, Africans, Asians, Melanesians, and Pacific Islanders immigrated to the Americas and they sometimes left their own communities to live among the indigenous peoples. Sometimes their survival depended upon being accepted into indigenous communities.

For those who adopt America's indigenous life ways in the modern era their fascination frequently takes the form of what scholars call *cultural appropriation.* Some people confuse acculturation with cultural appropriation and the other way around. Acculturation is not the same; it involves the process of adaptation by a person from one culture to another culture—this process is quite normal and may result in a significant cultural transformation. Many immigrants to the Americas became acculturated due to dependence on indigenous communities for personal survival or as a choice of cross-cultural immersion. They literally became integral parts of the indigenous community. Cultural appropriation, however, occurs when a person appropriates or engages in a pretense of knowledge or material appearance drawn from another culture for personal aggrandizement, social influence, or economic gain. Pretending to conduct spiritual practices from an indigenous culture, wearing regalia, invoking healing powers through dance, song, story or other means, sometimes for commercial purposes is cultural appropriation. It is particularly prevalent in the New Age movement when some individuals offer themselves as spiritual leaders or healers. Descendants of settlers can be guilty of cultural appropriation, as can individuals who are descendants of indigenous communities—New Age Indians. Such impostors may attract followings by unsuspecting individuals.

Few issues are as controversial or hurtful for indigenous Americans as the appropriation of their spiritual practices or their material wealth. From their perspective, the taking of spiritual traditions violates natural laws—the violation of which affects all human beings. There is also the realization that appropriating spiritual practices for personal gain is similar to stealing land: one more thing that is being taken without securing consent. Spiritual traditions and life ways, like land, are meaningful for human use. An individual, family or a whole community can hold such possessions. Personal possessions, as in personal spiritual knowledge, are gifts that can only be shared when a person decides to do so. Family knowledge may be only for the family or, if shared, only with the authorization of the family. Community knowledge is essentially public but demanding of respect by outsiders. This is essentially a scale of ethical practice where respect at each level is primary.

But there is more to it than that. The world's original cultures (and their spiritual traditions) evolved over thousands of years in conditions specific to each distinct people. They are based on their irreplaceable creation stories, or what peoples commonly call their original instructions—given to them by the Creator, based on the places they historically inhabited and their languages. Their cultural practices are inseparable from all of those conditions. They are given to the people to ensure their continuation as a healthy community.

When people from another society "borrow" from those traditions they take them out of the context for which they were intended. They are then cast through a different metaphysical lens, one that emphasizes the importance of the individual, the material and their sense of entitlement to those cultural assets.

Western European, Asian, Melanesian, African cultures and indigenous American cultures, while rooted in very different worldviews, can also be shared or exchanged in many ways. As we proceed through our explorations in this book we will explore exercises and the construction of rituals which, while shared through a culturally specific lens, will have a universal foundation or lesson for human change and growth.

LIFE'S NODES

In our work with clients we often notice that their voices change or their posture changes and they seem to be speaking from another time in their life. Often when people have been through powerful experiences either traumatic or positive—they leave a part of themselves in that time and place. When they talk about it, their consciousness returns there. In the case of traumatic events, they may have left part of themselves, like a limb of a tree that, when pruned, no longer grows from that branch, yet sprouts another.

One of the most potent ways to access these influences with our clients (and ourselves) is to complete the following worksheet. It provides a map of "nodes" or "knots" that connect or communicate. Once connected, they lead to greater meaning of one's map of life.

LIFE NODES

Directions: Please fill out the following worksheet.

List 5 moments from your past that are the most important times or events in your life.

1. _____

2. _____

3. _____

4. _____

5. _____

What aspects of these events are important?

_____

_____

_____

_____

Think about your immediate and extended family members (parents, siblings, grandparents, uncles, aunts, etc.). What roles did each of them play in the three most important events?

_____

_____

_____

_____

Are they aware of the importance of this event in your life?

_____

_____

_____

_____

RITUAL AND CULTURE

Rituals are found across all cultures and religions. Rituals organize behavior. Ritual behavior is defined as patterned, repetitive and rhythmic. Rituals are a form of psychological and physiological self-regulation. How we sit down to eat is a ritual; birthing and dying organize our entry and departure in the world and how we, heal and counsel include rituals that are reenacted each time we connect with a client or patient.

Sometimes rituals take over the individual--as in obsessive-compulsive disorder or addiction. Drug and alcohol use is a ritual, tobacco use is a ritual, as are tattoos and self-injury. Whether they are therapeutic or harmful depends on the individual, the set and setting, and purpose of the ritual. The practice of healing becomes a ritual when the sacred is embraced

Secular, cultural and spiritual healing are increasingly integrated into mental health and medical treatment. In addition to Judeo-Christian and Eastern cultural religious and healing practices, a variety of medical-spiritual rituals, are practiced today for mental health. These practices from cultures around the world can teach us about integrating spirituality with individual and community healing.

Ritual activities may include soul retrieval, trance dance, drumming ceremonies, fire-walking, vision quests, and entheogen use for healing from addictions. A variety of medical-spiritual rituals, practiced today for mental health include wilderness adventures, the American Indian (Lakota) sweat lodge, and shamanic "soul retrieval." For example, Hmong people who were refugees from Cambodia and Laos and live in California, Minnesota, Wisconsin, and North Carolina use spiritual practices including shamanic rituals. American Indian veterans may practice peyote ceremonies in the Native American Church, while Mexican *curandero/as* treat PTSD in Hispanic women and men using *limpias* (spiritual cleansings). Yoga is a ritual, rooted in Hindu practice that has become "secularized' making it acceptable to many peoples regardless of their religion. Thus rituals change and shift just as cultures do.

Of concern to us as clinicians are the ways rituals heal and also when ritual practices are not shared with clinicians in the office setting. While it is not always necessary for an individual or family to share their rituals, because they may wish to keep them private, more often people do not share because they feel they will be chastised or not understood or perhaps even reported to authorities.

Some rituals may seem foreign, strange or even pathological when seen in context of the ritual of a DSM-directed diagnostic and treatment approach. For example, among aboriginal culture in Australia, women cut themselves to express their grief. Some practices, like female and male circumcision, are condoned by many cultures and religions (Muslim sects and Jews respectively) but castigated by others.

In order to understand the role of ritual and to integrate it more actively in our work, we benefit from considering our own relationship to ritual.

CULTURAL RITUALS

Consider the role of ritual in your life. Many people grow up with meaningful rituals, and some experience attending rituals in form but with little experience or understanding of the meaning of the ritual. We often reject rituals we grew up with and replace them with others. Some are part of formal practices and others evolve with friends or families. Rituals made conscious become powerful tools for self-regulation.

Much of the stress and trauma of transitioning from one location to another, as refugees or immigrants do, is rooted in the loss of ritual.

There is often a lack of meaningful ritual for adolescents, the traditional time of life where one formally passes from childhood in adulthood. Or the original meaning and purpose behind rituals may be obscured by the "party" or materialism that can be associated with coming of age rituals like the *bar mitvah*, or the sweet 15 party called *a quinceañera* in Latino cultures.

CULTURAL RITUALS

Directions: Think about rituals you've practiced throughout your lifetime.

Did you grow up with rituals? Do you have pleasant, neutral, or negative memories? Explore three of them here.

1. _____

2. _____

3. _____

If you do not have any rituals that you practice or have practiced, what do you remember about the cultural, healing or ritual traditions of your grandparents?

_____

_____

_____

How did those early experiences inform your current attitudes and feelings?

_____

_____

_____

Do you currently have rituals that you engage in individually or within a group setting? What are they?

_____

_____

_____

Are there some rituals you would like to explore but have been embarrassed to or afraid of? What are they?

_____

_____

_____

Why are you feeling the way you do? What might you do to reach your goal?

_____

_____

_____

Think back on your own cultural and religious rituals. How might those rituals appear to someone who is unfamiliar with them?

_____

_____

_____

Do you conduct rituals with clients?

_____

_____

_____

What types of rituals can you imagine might be helpful for your clients?

_____

_____

_____

What rituals might you not conduct yourself, but refer to another facilitator to conduct?

_____

_____

_____

What rituals would make you uncomfortable?

_____

_____

_____

SACRED OBJECTS

This exercise is a simple but powerful step to incorporating the role of ritual or sacred objects. In psychology we often think of transitional objects that bring comfort to children or in times of stress. Sacred objects may have been a gift from a family member and serve as a lodestone. Sacred or ceremonial objects reflect a later stage of development where particular objects may be used to concentrate spiritual energy, to connect with higher powers, or to provide a visual cue or reminder of the essential self. This exercise provides an opportunity to explore and discuss deeper meaning with a client. If you have not done this yourself, this exercise is a profound way to deepen connection with family, friends and colleagues alike.

Directions: Ask your client to collect six items, as described below, that are important to them and bring them in (or show a photo). They may be made of any material and be significant in any way. Have your client explain why they chose each item and what it means to them.

- 1 item reflects who you are
- 1 item reflects your mother or your father
- 1 item reflects your cultural identity
- 1 item reflects a challenge in your life that you have overcome
- 1 item reflects your resilience and strength
- 1 item reflects your future

CULTURAL SUITCASE

Directions: Guide the client through the following visualization.

> *You are going on a long trip around the world. You can carry ten items with you that represent your cultural heritage.*

- *Describe each of the items.*

- *Which item(s) would you be willing to give away?*

- *Why will you give this item away?*

- *What does it mean to you to give it to someone?*

BIASES

What we believe is often a result of conditioning and exposure. As we explore our own identity and competency we need to explore the sources of our own biases and prejudices. The following introductory exercise is adapted from Dr. Heeson Jun's 2009 book, *Social Justice, Multicultural Counseling, and Practice: Beyond a Conventional Approach.* These provide us the opportunity to think through the kinds of biases we were exposed to and the ways in which they continue to influence us today.

BIASES

Directions: Answer the following questions alone, with a partner, or small group.

List three cultural/ethnic biases that were present in your home growing up:

1. _____

2. _____

3. _____

How old were you when you first became aware of these biases?

_____

_____

_____

Who shared these biases or comments/ideas? Mother/Father? Grandmother, Grandfather? Sibling?

_____

_____

_____

What were the ways these biases were communicated to you?

_____

_____

_____

How do you feel about these biases now?

_____

_____

_____

_____

If you released these biases when did you and why?

_____

_____

If you still carry some full or partial belief in these biases, can you explore this?

_____

_____

_____

List three religious/spiritual biases that you observed or heard:

1. _____

2. _____

3. _____

When did you realize that they were biases?

_____

_____

_____

What are your relationships to these biases now?

_____

_____

_____

Describe the sociocultural and political context of your childhood.

_____

_____

_____

_____

STEREOTYPES

Stereotype is the unfair belief that all people or things with a particular characteristic are the same. "Unfair" implies characteristics perceived as inherently negative, and potentially stigmatizing.

Stereotyping is related to stigmatization because the sense of inherent inferiority that drives it can result in lumping people into categories (usually derisively) that don't accurately reflect who they are. Consider all the pejorative terms used to describe people with mental illness: crazy, insane, retarded, retard, psycho, nuts, schizo, or lunatic.

Below is a list of stereotypes common to various groups:

African Americans—lazy; hyper-sexual; gang members or other kinds of criminals; all single mothers are on welfare and sponge off the system

American Indians—all are alcoholics; stupid; lazy; live on reservations; they have vanished; not authentic if not full-blooded

Latinos—all Spanish-speakers are Mexican; all are "illegal aliens"; gang members or other kinds of criminals; built for physical labor; sponge off the system; men are chauvinists

Asians—all Asians are "Oriental" (i.e. they all look alike); they are all inherently smarter than everyone else; bad drivers; men are chauvinists; bad at athletics; all are martial artists

Arab Americans—terrorists; belly dancers; billionaires; American enemies; oppressive toward women

Euromericans—have no history; can't cook; have no rhythm; drink too much; self-absorbed; all are wealthy; uneducated about people other than themselves, uptight, stiff upper lip

Pacific Islanders—they are Asians; they are all Hawaiians; all Pacific Islanders are Polynesian; good football players; dancers; exotic; big

Christians—bigots; hypocritical; judgmental; intolerant; conservative; self-righteous; superior

Muslims—all Muslims are terrorists; all Arabs are Muslims; all Muslims are Arabs; Sikhs are Muslims; all Muslims are intolerant toward other religions; Muslims are savages; women have no rights

Jews—men are effeminate and not good at sports; women are pushy; cheap

Buddhists—all Buddhists meditate; are pacifists and vegetarian

Hindu—all Hindus worship idols and cows; are vegetarians; support a social caste system

Lesbians—man-haters; were molested as children; they just haven't found the right guy; all lesbian relationships have a "butch" and a "femme"; hyper-sexual

Gay Men—all gay men are effeminate; flamboyant; hyper-sexual and promiscuous; not relationship oriented; HIV/AIDS is a gay disease; gay men are pedophiles; homosexuality is caused by childhood trauma or abuse; gay couples can't raise healthy children

Transgender—all drag queens and kings are gay; transgender people are perverts; butch lesbians are transgender; all people who dress as the opposite sex are homosexual

People with Disabilities—they are partial or limited people, thus "different"; the successful "handicapped" person is superhuman; disability is a sickness, something to be fixed; people with disabilities are a menace to others, to themselves, to society; people with disabilities, especially cognitive impairments, are holy innocents endowed with special grace, with the function of inspiring others to value life

STEREOTYPES

Directions: Close your eyes and allow your stream of consciousness to flow, what are the first words that rise to your awareness when you think of *(insert specific group or population)*. List those words below.

_____	_____	_____
_____	_____	_____
_____	_____	_____
_____	_____	_____
_____	_____	_____
_____	_____	_____
_____	_____	_____
_____	_____	_____
_____	_____	_____
_____	_____	_____
_____	_____	_____

STIGMATIZATION AND SELF-STIGMA

Stigmatization involves applying negative judgments to people who have physical or social characteristics as conditions of their life they didn't choose (such as mental illness). Stigmatization refers to social marginalization, even to the point of discrimination at the group or institutional level. This may include blaming, shaming, name-calling, ridicule, social exclusion, and condescension.

Stigmatizing behaviors allow people to distance themselves from others they deem somehow inferior to themselves. For people with mental health issues, social stigmatization can be one of the biggest barriers to securing help that they need. It also increases the risk of homelessness, group ostracism and other forms of victimization.

Stigmatization in turn leads to "self-stigma" in three stages: (1) people become aware of the stereotype, (2) they agree with it and (3) then identify with it. This leads to reduced self-confidence, self-esteem, a sense of worthlessness, and loss of belief in oneself. Self-stigmatizing can result in an inability to seek education opportunities, hold a job, or maintain family and other social connections.

Double Stigma

Double stigma refers to people who may be stigmatized because of several aspects of their lives, for example: mental illness and sexual identity, mental illness and physical illness, mental illness and ethnicity.

Stigma and self-stigma may be more severe in certain types of illnesses, cultural/ethnic groups or among certain identities, such as gay, lesbian and transsexual.

Keys to Overcome Stigma

We explore stigmatization with a client to review current and past hurts, and to understand stigma as a social issue that often becomes internalized. Stigma gets in the way of healing. It often begins as social stigma, or stigma enforced in the family and then it becomes self-stigma. Only by airing the experiences of stigmatization and taking action does stigma become transformed. The myth exercise done previously can be revisited to explore and deepen understanding of how the hero wrestles with and ultimately overcomes stigma.

One of the things we do as care providers is to help our clients become aware of their self-stigmatization and help them overcome it. The key to recovery from stigmatization is empowerment. Transforming stigma into action. We have seen this occur for example with consumer and advocacy groups like the National Alliance on Mental Illness (NAMI) (https://www.nami.org/)

The following pages are exercises to help transform self-stigmatization into more empowering life experiences. These exercises work best when done over a course of a few weeks or months, observing how the client's thoughts and ideas change as they work to overcome stigma.

SELF-STIGMA

Directions: Fill out the worksheet to help you identify how you relate to stigma.

Please name some words that you would apply to yourself about your mental health issues:

_____

_____

_____

If those words include some negative or stigmatizing terms, please take a moment to feel how those words make you feel and find some words to express those feelings:

_____

_____

_____

Identify where these terms originated:

_____

_____

_____

_____

When did your first hear them?

_____

_____

_____

_____

Are they words or names you have been called?

_____

_____

_____

_____

Are they names that society uses in general?

_____

_____

_____

_____

How long have you been carrying these words, names, this stigma?

_____

_____

_____

_____

Are there family members who also carry this stigma or a similar one?

_____

_____

_____

_____

Do you have family members or friends that you do not reveal information to about yourself because of this stigma?

_____

_____

_____

_____

CHANGING SELF-STIGMATIZTION

Once your client has explored how they have internalized family or socially generated stigma, they can work on reframing and releasing those thoughts and ideas. This can be done through daily exercises designed to change negative thought patterns into a more positive self-image.

Directions: Ask your client the following questions.

- *How do you want to be seen?*

- *What are the qualities you aspire to?*

- *What qualities do you see in yourself?*

- *Distill it down to single words or phrases.*

Client Homework Assignment

Ask your client to write down qualities they identified in the exercise on sticky notes and leave them in places where they will see them daily such as the bathroom mirror or refrigerator. For at least one month they will look at these notes every day and work at internalizing those qualities.

Cognitive behavioral therapies individually or in a group format, have been shown to be effective for reducing self-stigma. Increasing self-esteem and self-efficacy is foundational to self-stigma recovery.

For an amusing and poignant look at empathy, watch:
https://www.thersa.org/discover/videos/rsa-shorts/2013/12/Brene-Brown-on-Empathy/

ETHICAL STANDARDS FOR CULTURALLY COMPETENT PRACTICE

As clinicians and mental health practitioners, we all adhere to our organization codes of ethics; it may be the American Psychological Association's (APA) code of ethics, or the American Counseling Association (ACA) or the National Association of Social Workers' (NASW) code of ethics. Increasingly these codes are expanding definitions to address the diversity of an individual's culture, abilities, and religions, sexual and gender identity and orientations.

Cultural competency also includes linguistic awareness and competency. This leads to awareness of how diverse languages and accents affect clinical interactions and may lead to the need for translators. Ethics also requires that we are aware of the needs of diverse clients and how to make referrals. These may vary from voice coaching for transgender individuals who seek to transition their voices to match their gender identity and gender expression to individuals who are hearing-impaired who need voice support.

Yet in spite of our best training we will always encounter new and challenging ethical questions that may require supervision or consultation. The next worksheets include some areas to explore about ethics and culture that can illumine new areas for growth and skill development.

CODE OF ETHICS

Directions: Please answer the following questions.

Have you ever experienced a mismatch between the cultural care needs of your clients and your code of ethics? In what way?

_____

_____

_____

If you were a member of the team contributing to the ethics codes of your organization, what values do you feel should be included?

_____

_____

_____

Has a client ever asked for a response from you or an intervention that is culturally appropriate for them but less so, or not at all so, for you based on how you felt or how the codes are defined?

_____

_____

_____

How might your responses be different now than in the past?

_____

_____

_____

_____

DIVERSITY AND BOUNDARIES

Competency compels us to recognize the effects of diversity boundaries.

Intellectual or physical gifts, feelings about physical closeness, medications, religious attitudes, politics, what we share about feelings, how important punctuality is and appointments, touch, and more.

Social boundaries between individuals and groups pose a challenge for clinicians and understanding the various types of boundaries as well as the social consequences if those boundaries are inadvertently violated is crucial to one's professional effectiveness. Cultural competency aids us in our ability to bridge boundaries or avoid violating boundaries.

DIVERSITY AND BOUNDARIES

Directions: Please answer the following questions.

What are your values about boundaries in your personal life?

_____

_____

_____

_____

_____

What are your values about boundaries with your clients/patients?

_____

_____

_____

_____

_____

How do you feel about receiving gifts from a client?

_____

_____

_____

_____

_____

Copyright 2016 © Leslie E. Korn, *Multicultural Counseling Workbook*. All Rights Reserved

CASE VIGNETTE: NNAKEME

You have worked with Nnakeme for six months during his migration transition from Nigeria. You are preparing to terminate when he brings you a gift; an elaborate dress with beads and jewels. He hands it to you and says he is most appreciative of your work together and he wants to share a gift with you. He says that where he comes from, a gift is always given to a healer who has helped another.

Which would you choose?

A.   Thank you Nnakeme, but I cannot accept this gift. I do not accept gifts from clients.

B.   Thank you Nnakeme, I think this is a beautiful dress and I will treasure it.

C.   Thank you Nnakeme, I am sorry but my code of ethics prevents me from accepting this gift.

D.   Thank you Nnakeme. I am so appreciative of this gift. I will accept this because I know that it is in your tradition to give a gift to a healer. In my tradition as a therapist, we do not accept gifts. However, we have worked for six months and during this time I have worked to understand your culture just as you have mine and in keeping in that spirit I am honored to accept your gift.

Why did you respond the way you did?

_____

_____

_____

_____

_____

_____

_____

_____

_____

_____

RESOURCES

Access many of these resources online at www.healthalt.org

Books & Publications
Rastogi, M., Massey-Hastings, N., & Wieling, E. (2012). Barriers to Seeking Mental Health Services in the Latino/a Community: A Qualitative Analysis. In *Journal of Systemic therapies, Vol. 31, No. 4*, pp. 1-17.

Movies/Videos
A Tale of Mental Illness—From The Inside
Ted Talk by lawyer Elyn Saks who lives with schizophrenia: found on YouTube

What's So Funny About Mental Illness?
Ted Talk by comedian Ruby Wax about her mental illness
http://www.ted.com/talks/ruby_wax_what_s_so_funny_about_mental_illness?language=en

Saving Face: Recognizing and Managing the Stigma of Mental Illness in Asian Americans
https://ethnomed.org/clinical/mental-health/SavingFace.flv/view

Organizations
Bring Change 2 Mind
Their mission is to end the stigma and discrimination surrounding mental illness through widely distributed public education materials based on the latest scientific insights and measured for effectiveness. Lots of great educational PSA's videos and stories on their website.
http://bringchange2mind.org/learn/choose-your-words/

World Health Organization (WHO)
International resource for clinicians, providing policy papers, publications and exposure to the international mandates for mental health. This is especially useful for those who work internationally and for accessing statistics and demographics.
http://www.who.int/mental_health/en/

Web Resources
Ethics Codes: Access this book's website to download the ethical codes of conduct for:
        American Counseling Association
        National Association of Social Workers
        American Nurses Association
        American Psychological Association

Family Heritage and Name Meanings
Offers DNA testing and personal health info: https://www.23andme.com/user/signup/
Trace the ancestry of people of African descent: http://www.africanancestry.com/home/
Search for ancestry coming through Ellis Island: http://www.ellisisland.org/
Access original military records: http://www.fold3.com/
International genealogy links: http://www.genealogylinks.net/

Chapter 2
Racism and Racial Prejudice

Chapter 2
Racism and Racial Prejudice

*"Racial inequalities in health exist across a range of biological systems
among adults and are not explained by racial differences in poverty.
The weathering effects of living in a race-conscious society may be greatest
among those Blacks most likely to engage in high-effort coping."*

— Arline T. Geronimus, Margaret Hicken,
Danya Keene, and John Bound, *American Journal of Public Health*

We now turn to a review of concepts and attitudes about race—that often used term that refers to outward appearances. We will practice exercises that address interpersonal and institutional experiences, micro-aggression and concepts of privilege. Definitions of race, ethnicity, white fragility, color blindness, color consciousness and cultural transference are discussed at length. Through several exercises we consider the effects of stress and discrimination on mental and physical health. These are especially useful for the clinician to complete with the client. I also share exercises that enhance our understanding and our competency to work with people who experience the uncertainties of immigration, alienation and forced dislocation as refugees.

Personal and social oppression affect physical and mental well-being.

- *What do we need to know about that to improve our work with clients?*
- *How do we deepen our understanding of our own internalized oppression as well as our privileged status and their effect on our relationships?*

ALLOSTATIC LOAD, RACISM, AND BIGOTRY

Allostatic load is the effect of chronic stress on the body and mind. It is the "wear and tear" effect that results from chronic stressors in daily life. Allostatic load leads to stress and physical illness. How can we define this process more fully with clients in the context of cultural practices? How then can we enhance factors that will be protective and support resilience?

As clinicians, we frequently focus on helping our clients cope with the stress of daily life and we use various methods to reduce stress. **Most of our clients experience added chronic stress due to their identity or how others perceive them.** Stress affects their ability to function in society based on their ethnic, cultural or minority identities.

Multiple factors have an effect on a client's presenting problems and subsequent healing or recovery. Some factors make individuals more vulnerable to psychological discomfort while others help to buffer them. These are referred to as *risk and protective factors*. Disenfranchised or marginalized individuals, such as ethnic minorities, women, and individuals with disabilities can greatly benefit from being able to openly discuss these factors in counseling and gain better understanding of the influence they can have on mental health. Identifying and understanding risk and protective factors, as well as the processes through which they operate, are also important to clinicians. Such knowledge contributes to a more all-inclusive depiction of individuals and their environments. It also assists in building therapeutic relationships between clinicians and clients that are based on mutual understanding of current challenges, as well as strengths that can contribute to positive clinical outcomes.

You may complete the following exercise in order to explore your own history and level of chronic stress or risk of allostatic load. Then, you can give these worksheets to your client to fill out. They can be reviewed together in order to explore the concept and specifics of allostatic load, and also to identify and enhance protective factors.

ALLOSTATIC LOAD

Directions: Please answer the following questions.

There are many chronic stressors in modern life:

- Poverty
- Race
- Disability
- Sexism
- Harassment

- Ethnicity
- Caregiving
- Migration
- Lack of healthcare
- Work

Name a few chronic stressors you have observed or experienced:

_____

_____

_____

_____

_____

List the stressors you experienced until the age of 21:

_____

_____

_____

_____

_____

List the stressors you experienced post age 21 through the present:

_____

_____

_____

_____

"Ism's" are Stressors

Racism is a stressor; it leads to chronic autonomic arousal, which can result in:

- Depression
- Hypertension
- Diabetes type 2
- Self-medicating addictive behaviors

NOTE: African Americans have higher early mortality compared to non-Hispanic whites. It is believed to be due to the effects of racism in the U.S. (Mays, Cochran, & Barnes, (2007)

Do you know someone who experiences discrimination or bigotry and is at risk for allostatic load? Why?

_____

_____

_____

_____

_____

_____

_____

What other minority groups are at risk for allostatic load?

_____

_____

_____

_____

_____

_____

_____

RISK AND PROTECTIVE FACTORS: CARD SORT

This exercise can be used to enhance client participation in treatment planning by exploring risk and protective factors, as well as processes through which they operate. This exercise is rooted in a multicultural approach to counseling that recognizes, respects, and responds to client diversity. It also fosters self-awareness and helps clinicians and clients move from problem-focused to solution-focused approaches to healing and recovery.

Materials: You can print out 25 cards (as shown on page 48) from go.pesi.com/multicultural or design your own.

Directions:

1. Ask the client to look through all of the cards to get an overall sense of the options available.

2. Instruct client to eliminate 10 cards that least influence current symptoms or challenges that brought them to counseling. The clinician must be prepared to define all terms and provide support in completing this task.

3. From the remaining 15 cards, clients are to select the top five that have the most influence on current symptoms or the challenges that brought them to counseling. This task might cause some clients to feel pulled between certain choices. Clinicians are to encourage clients to take their time and remember that this process should reflect influences on current symptoms or challenges they are experiencing right now.

4. Client narrows their selection to the top three influences. This step may be even more difficult than the previous one. If needed, clinicians are to explain that life is fluid, and selections from this card sort activity can change over time. Influences that are predominant today may be different from those that existed a few weeks, months, or even years ago. Today's most predominant influences could also change in the future.

5. After clients have completed their selections, ask them to reflect on the following items. Use client responses to provoke serious self-reflection.

   a. the first 10 cards that were easy to eliminate

   b. cards that were challenging to discard out of the next 15

   c. the top 5 cards and how the final three most influence current symptoms or challenges

6. Wrap up the discussion by emphasizing which cards are risk versus protective factors or processes. Further distinguish between these as negative versus positive influences. Focus on protective factors and processes for use in treatment planning.

• Cards that are eliminated may consist of protective factors or processes the client is not readily aware of. Make note of these for discussion and potential use in treatment planning.

• The cards provided for this activity are not an exhaustive list for completing this exercise. Clinicians are encouraged to remove or add cards that are as specific as possible to a client's culture, ethnicity, worldview, etc.

This game was developed by Dr. Keitha Wright and is used here with her permission.

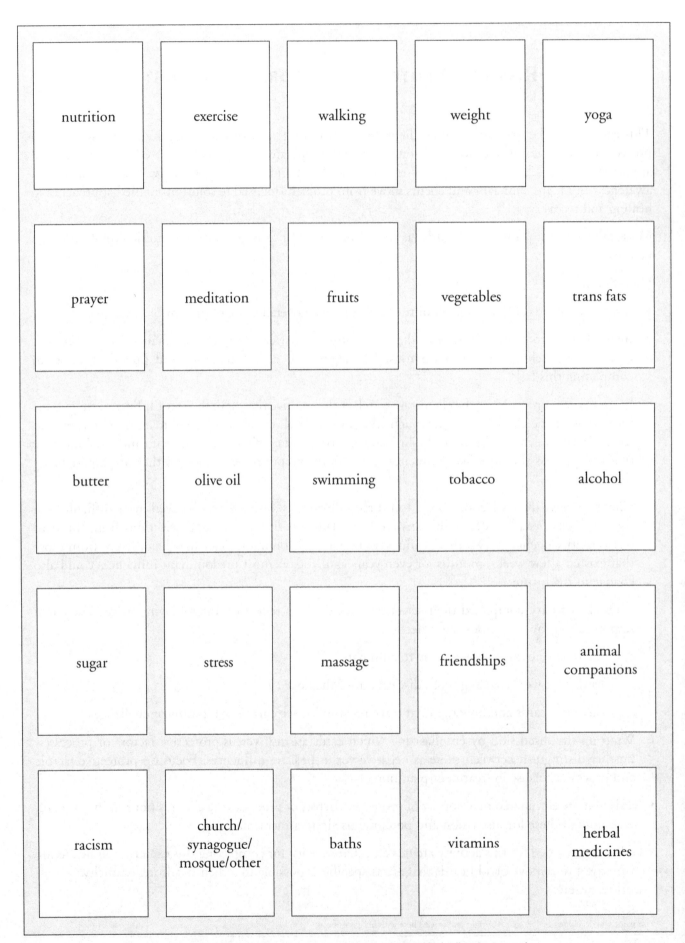

nutrition	exercise	walking	weight	yoga
butter	olive oil	swimming	tobacco	alcohol
prayer	meditation	fruits	vegetables	trans fats
sugar	stress	massage	friendships	animal companions
racism	church/ synagogue/ mosque/other	baths	vitamins	herbal medicines

RISK AND PROTECTIVE FACTORS

We cannot always change the external stressors or risk factors but we can incorporate protective factors. There are risk and protective factors that intersect with physical health.

Directions: Please fill out the worksheet.

Risk Factors

Identify three risk factors you experience:

1. _____

2. _____

3. _____

Protective Factors

Identify three protective factors you experience:

1. _____

2. _____

3. _____

Choose a protective factor you have considered adding in your self-care.

_____

_____

_____

What are the obstacles to engaging this protective factor?

_____

_____

_____

What or who can help you overcome these obstacles?

_____

_____

_____

This worksheet is used with the permission of Dr. Keitha Wright.

CODE-SWITCHING AND IDENTITY

Did you grow up in family where English was not predominantly spoken? Did you grow up in a community where everyone spoke a different dialect of English compared to the formal English you were taught in school? If so, you probably learned early on that in your home or community environment there was one way of communicating, while in the "outside world" there was another way of communicating—to which you had to adapt.

Linguists call this adaptation code-switching. It suggests that identity is formed as a result not just of pre-determined social categories like class, socioeconomic status, ethnicity, class, or gender, but through ways people interact with others. We code-switch to signify our membership in a particular group, and to signify our exclusion from other groups.

We may also "switch" to demonstrate our allegiance to a group in which we may not actually be a member. For example, in Hawaii, locals (defined there as people of Hawaiian ethnicity) grew up speaking pidgin, a creole dialect of English that can be very difficult for those not fluent in pidgin to understand. Non-Hawaiian residents who speak pidgin do so to indicate their alliance with the locals in order to gain acceptance based (at least loosely) on Hawaiian notions of belonging.

Code-switching responds to a range of dynamics that can be as subtle as connecting to someone by using a word or phrase only someone in that particular group would understand. Or it might be more overt, such as dropping an accent in social circumstances when there is a perceived need to fit in.

As a clinician, knowing what code-switching is and why people do it enhances cultural competency. The following exercises are designed to increase your awareness of ways you might have grown up code-switching and not known you were doing it, or to help you become aware of when other people are doing it and why.

Examples of Code-Switching

One of the best ways to understand code-switching is to see it in action. President Barack Obama, for instance, earned enough of a reputation for code-switching that comedians Key and Peele satirized him in this video of a fictitious presidential meet and greet. https://www.youtube.com/watch?v=nopWOC4SRm4

In another candid video, President Obama is code-switching while ordering a chili dog at a counter in a packed fast food restaurant: https://www.youtube.com/watch?v=N5fWeVzQnZ4

Key and Peele captured another funny but poignant instance of code-switching in this 48 second video: https://www.youtube.com/watch?v=JzprLDmdRlc

Watch George Lopez on Spanglish: https://www.youtube.com/watch?v=Z13CVD0idrM

Code Switching

In my own clinical practice I work with both English and Spanish-speaking adults. I notice that bilingual adults code-switch with me throughout our sessions together. They take the lead in changing languages and I follow their lead and together we move back and forth. I notice that they may switch for a variety of reasons: they may be better able to express their feelings in Spanish, or the content may be particularly meaningful or fraught with emotional sensitivity and meaning. Whatever reasons each client may choose to switch at each point in time, I notice that it deepens our bonds as we move between languages and improves our capacity to understand the other.

CODE-SWITCHING IN YOUR FAMILY

Directions: The following questions can be discussed with a friend, colleague or used with a client in session.

- *Did you grow up in a family where English was not a first language in your generation, your parents', or grandparents' generations?*

- *Do you have memories of you or your parents/grandparents having to adjust their language to blend in to mainstream society?*

- *Describe your memories of how language was negotiated in your family.*

- *Did you have a perception of being "different" from other kids you knew?*

- *What kinds of feelings do you remember having about your family's ethnicity?*

- *Were there other families with similar ethnicities and languages where you grew up?*

- *How have your perceptions changed over time?*

- *Are you aware of yourself code-switching?*

- *If you aren't from a family where English isn't a first language, perhaps you know other people who are. Think of someone you may be close to who is bilingual or who is from a bilingual family.*

- *Have you ever noticed them alternating between languages (or perhaps dialects), maybe in one conversation or even mid-sentence?*

- *What might be the motivator for the switching?*

EVERYDAY DISCRIMINATION

"We define racism as an institutionalized system of economic, political, social, and cultural relations that ensures that one racial group has and maintains power and privilege over all others in all aspects of life. Individual participation in racism occurs when the objective outcome of behavior reinforces these relations, regardless of the subjective intent."

— Carol Brunson Phillips and Louise Derman-Sparks
Authors of *Teaching/Learning Anti-Racism: A Developmental Approach*

Microaggression

Microaggression refers to the casual degradation of whole classes of people, for example, minorities, women, religious groups, people with disabilities, in ways that are often unconscious. Subtle or not, microaggressions are hurtful and discriminatory.

There are at least three forms of Microaggression:

Microinsult — A microinsult is rudeness or insensitivity that demeans a person's racial heritage or identity. They are often subtle snubs that convey a hidden insulting message.

Microinvalidation — Communications that exclude, negate, or nullify the psychological thoughts, feelings, or experiential reality of another.

Microassault — An explicit verbal or nonverbal attack meant to hurt a person using name-calling, avoidant behaviour, and discriminatory actions.

Media Example of Microinsult and Microinvalidation

The TV show "Scandal" is about a Washington D.C. "fixer," Olivia Pope, who is the CEO of her firm. Olivia Pope is an African American woman. In one scene, Olivia enters the room of a client, walking side by side with her team. Walking next to her is a white woman; the client walks directly up to the white woman and introduces herself to the white woman, assuming that she is Olivia Pope, the president of the firm, at which point the real Olivia Pope says smiling, "I am Olivia Pope."

CASE VIGNETTES: MICROAGGRESSION

Microinvalidation

I had a long-time acquaintance who I knew prior to knowing my husband. One day I introduced them and she said to him: "You don't look like an Indian."

How would you respond in my position?

_____

_____

Microinsult

Once I was receiving a therapeutic massage. I knew the therapist well and thus we were chatting a bit. She was sharing with me about her purchases of used cars, when she said: "I always tried to Jew them down." I was on the table, clothes off, and supposed to be relaxing. I said nothing, but could feel myself become tense. I decided to wait until later to say something to her. Later we talked and she explained that she did not realize that it was an offensive remark. She had grown up in rural Washington and had never met a Jewish person.

How would you respond in my position?

_____

_____

Microassault

Dr. Chester Pierce, an African American psychiatrist born in 1927, defined and developed the concept of microaggression. Dr. Derald Wing Sue has further elucidated it. I studied behavioral health with Dr. Pierce as a graduate student at the Harvard School of Public Health in the mid 1980's. It was a small class and during the first meeting we were all introducing ourselves, and an individual who was a physician from Jamaica said, as part of his introduction: "The Jews control Jamaica, just as they control all the banks." I sat there stunned not believing that I had heard him correctly. I said nothing as my mind scrambled to make sense of what I had heard.

How would you respond in my position?

_____

_____

EXERCISE
MICROAGGRESSION

Directions: Please answer the following questions.

How have you experienced a microassault, microinsult, and or microinvalidation?

_____

_____

_____

_____

_____

_____

_____

How have you delivered a microassault, microinsult, and/or microinvalidation?

_____

_____

_____

_____

_____

_____

_____

_____

SOCIAL PRIVILEGE

Since Peggy McIntosh's famous article about white privilege written in 1988, a body of literature about privilege has been growing. It recognizes that unearned privilege emerges out of interrelated hierarchies of power in all aspects of social life.

One can benefit from privilege based on class, citizenship, language, sexual orientation, gender, physical ability, and numerous other traits. From this perspective, discrimination is a matter of degree and is contextual. One can experience privilege in some aspects of life but not in others.

Allan Johnson coined the term "systems of privilege" in his book *Privilege, Power, and Difference* (2001). Systems of privilege can develop in families, workplaces, and society in general, and is organized around the principles of domination, identification, and centeredness. For example, "white" privilege is a system of privilege in which *whiteness* is centered and a default point, i.e. white people tend to occupy positions of power, exhibiting a form of unearned privilege.

> **Did you know?**
>
> - Privilege is usually invisible to those who possess it.
>
> - Privilege can come with things we take for granted, such as being able-bodied, heterosexual, or English-speaking.
>
> - One can be privileged in some ways but not in others.
>
> - People can receive social privileges whether or not they recognize or want them.

The "racialized" concept of "white" rests on physical appearance, and not social or cultural origins. As such, individuals may gain privileges based solely on their appearance, which results in a circumstance where an individual may "pass" despite having a quite different ethnic background that would otherwise disqualify. Privilege is also associated with economic accumulation, crossing color and ethnic barriers.

CHECK YOUR PRIVILEGE

The "Check Your Privilege" movement (largely an online phenomenon) has challenged people to individually become self-aware of the levels of privilege they enjoy. Scholars working with issues of diversity, race, class, and identity stress the difficulty people often experience identifying with difference, preferring to see themselves as "normal." Identifying our own privilege is a source of discomfort for many, making privilege all the more difficult to identify. It can engender feelings of guilt and shame to be associated with systems of oppression

Directions: Discuss and answer the following questions.

What does social privilege mean to you?

_____

_____

Is it related more to race, economics, or other factors?

_____

_____

Are you aware of people in your life who think of themselves as socially privileged based on their race or other attributes?

_____

_____

In what ways do you consider yourself a privileged (or unprivileged) person?

_____

_____

How does is make you feel?

_____

_____

How difficult or easy is it to talk about?

_____

_____

What is "White Privilege"?

While the concept of "white privilege" dates to the writings of W.E. DuBois in the 1930's, it came into more mainstream usage after Peggy McIntosh published *White Privilege: Unpacking the Invisible Knapsack."* The essay outlined a list of attributes that confer unearned privilege upon people by virtue of their skin color. It emphasized the idea that racism comprises more than acts of individual meanness, but rather is built into and functions in society systemically rendering it nearly invisible.

White privilege is an implied collection of benefits that attach to being a recognizable member of the dominant (white) culture. McIntosh's approach was to center on her identity as a "white person" to reflect on ways she possessed implicit social advantages because of her whiteness.

These included advantages such as

- Not being harassed because of her skin color
- Seeing images of people of her "race" as responsible for civilization
- Not being told she is a credit to her race based on her accomplishments

> **You can ask your client:**
> *Do you consider ways in which you might be socially privileged?*

In Eurocentric cultures we are taught that with hard work we can acquire the benefits associated with that hard work, including a well-paying job, the ability to own a house, a car, and other material comforts that go with financial security. Other benefits include social status that comes with education, heterosexuality, and Christianity; i.e. the ability not to be socially marginalized. Built into this paradigm is the implication that if you don't acquire these benefits of society it is because you didn't work hard enough for them (i.e. you didn't make the right choices), thus it is your own fault.

This is the way the invisibility of social privilege is maintained. It is masked by the presumption of innocence, cloaked in the language of hard work and personal choices. Believing that the social benefits one enjoys are acquired by the sweat of one's own brow, systems of inequality can be denied and guilt can be assuaged.

"Privilege" then becomes a dirty word no one wants any part of, because to be privileged is to deny the legitimizing effects of one's own efforts.

To check your own level of inherent social privilege, see this Buzzfeed.com quiz:
http://www.buzzfeed.com/regajha/how-privileged-are-you#.nfM01ABa70

WHITE PRIVILEGE

Directions: Please answer the following questions.

Do you use the term "white" or "Anglo"?

_____

_____

_____

What do these terms mean to you? Do you wonder which is "correct"?

_____

_____

_____

Are you aware of people in your life who think of themselves as privileged based on their whiteness?

_____

_____

_____

If you consider yourself a privileged person based on your whiteness, how does it make you feel? How difficult or easy is it to talk about?

_____

_____

_____

_____

White Fragility

The concept of white fragility complements the concept of white privilege. "Why is it so hard to talk to white people about racism?" asks Robin DiAngelo, a professor of critical multicultural and social justice education at Westfield State University in Massachusetts. She studies "whiteness" and has coined the term white fragility, which refers to: "a state in which even a minimum amount of racial stress becomes intolerable, triggering a range of defensive moves. These moves include outward display of emotions such as anger, fear and guilt, and behaviors such as argumentation, silence and leaving the stress-inducing situation."

The following are examples of the kinds of challenges that trigger racial stress for white people:

- Suggesting that a white person's viewpoint comes from a racialized frame of reference (challenge to objectivity);
- People of color talking directly about their own racial perspectives (challenge to white taboos on talking openly about race);
- People of color choosing not to protect the racial feelings of white people with regard to race (challenge to white racial expectations and need/entitlement to racial comfort);
- People of color not being willing to tell their stories or answer questions about their racial experiences (challenge to the expectation that people of color will serve us);
- A fellow white not providing agreement with one's racial perspective (challenge to white solidarity);
- Receiving feedback that one's behavior had a racist impact (challenge to white racial innocence);
- Suggesting that group membership is significant (challenge to individualism);
- An acknowledgment that access is unequal among racial groups (challenge to meritocracy);
- Being presented with a person of color in a position of leadership (challenge to white authority);
- Being presented with information about other racial groups through, for example, movies in which people of color drive the action but are not in stereotypical roles, or multicultural education (challenge to white centrality).

The work of writers and scholars of white privilege highlights the need for self-recognition of privilege. Some of the important points they make about white privilege include:

- Remember that white people weren't the first ones to begin talking about white privilege; people of color were.
- White privilege manifests daily in both public and private relationships.
- Anti-racism activism by whites is important, but it can also have harmful or counter-productive effects. For example when white people make a lot of money or gain fame from their anti-racism work, it can render invisible the perspectives of people of color.

 Ask your client:
"Do you consider ways in which your skin color accords you levels of privilege?"

MASS INCARCERATION OF PEOPLE OF COLOR

More people are imprisoned in the United States than in any other country in the world; and people of color constitute a disproportionate part of the incarcerated. Sixty percent of people imprisoned are from racial or ethnic minorities. According to the Sentencing Project, African American men have a one in three chance of being imprisoned, while Spanish-speaking men have a one in six chance of being imprisoned, compared to a one in seventeen chance of imprisonment for white Americans. American Indians are incarcerated at a rate 38% higher than than the national average, according to the U.S. Commission on Civil Rights. This is due to differential treatment by the criminal justice system, lack of access to adequate counsel and racial profiling.

Clinician Support and Advocacy

As clinicians, we are often called upon to support and treat people and their families during incarceration, upon release, and during parole.

Understanding the role of social injustices like racism, poverty and mental illness that contribute to in carceration is essential to effective clinical care. Yet we also search for ways to empower someone during and after incarceration that is solely under his or her control.

Unlocking the Mind While Being in Lock-up

One of the most profound approaches to supporting people in prison is the movement of Vipassana that is being introduced nationwide in correctional facilities. Vipassana, also known as mindfulness meditation means, "to see things as they really are." It is an ancient Buddhist technique of meditation. It is often applied as a non-sectarian approach to self-transformation through self-observation.

Research findings suggest that results in prison populations include the enhancement of psychological well-being, a decrease in substance use, and a decrease in recidivism.

Did you know?

The Dhamma Brothers is the story of the introduction of Vipassana meditation into a maximum-security prison in Alabama. Jenny Philips, a psychiatric nurse, filmed a documentary, about this powerful story of healing that may be viewed on Netflix.
Movie trailers may be viewed at: http://www.dhammabrothers.com/Trailer.htm

"For the first time, I could observe my pain and grief. I felt a tear fall. Then something broke, and I couldn't stop sobbing. I found myself in a terrain where I had always wanted to be, but never had a map. I found myself in the inner landscape, and now I had some direction."

— Omar Rahman, Dhamma Brother

RESOURCES:

Access many of these resources online at www.healthalt.org

Books and Publications

Bullock, B. E., & Toribio, A. J. (2012). The Cambridge Handbook of Linguistic Code-switching Cambridge Handbooks in Language and Linguistics. New York, NY: Cambridge University Press.

De Fina, A. (2007). *Code-Switching and the Construction of Ethnic Identity in a Community of Practice.* New York, NY: Cambridge University Press.

Delpit, L., & Dowdy, J. K. (2013). *Skin That We Speak: Thoughts on Language and Culture in the Classroom.* New York, NY: The New Press

Demby, G. (2013). *How Code-Switching Explains the World.*
http://www.npr.org/blogs/codeswitch/2013/04/08/176064688/how-code-switching-explains-the-world

Gardner-Chloros, P. (2009). *Code-Switching.* New York, NY: Cambridge University Press.

Wheeler, R. S., & Swords, R. S. (2010). *Code-Switching Lessons: Grammar Strategies for Linguistically Diverse Writers.* Westport Connecticut, CT: Greenwood Publishing Group.

Movies/Videos

The Dhamma Brothers
In this documentary film, psychiatric nurse/filmmaker Jenny Phillips tells the dramatic tale of human potential and transformation as she follows and documents the stories of the prison inmates at Donaldson Correctional Facility as they enter into an arduous and intensive program of Vipassana meditation training.

Watch George Lopez on Spanglish: https://www.youtube.com/watch?v=Z13CVD0idrM
Code Switching and Social Class: https://www.youtube.com/watch?v=4HIe4qwObUk

Dadaab Stories
Watch this interactive, multi-media documentary project charting everyday life in the world's largest refugee camp. Bringing together video, poetry, music, community journalism and individual blogs, Dadaab Stories is a living, curated collection of personal stories.
https://www.youtube.com/playlist?list=PLW_ORc1wzxdXyAiIxYM-Tx4HLkMI_4dlm

Organizations

Prison Dharma Project: Mindfulness in Prisons
http://www.prisonmindfulness.org/projects/network-directory/548/freedom-behind-bars/

This project also provides a toolkit on meditation which is available to download as PDF's at:
http://www.healthalt.org/mindfulness.html

The Prison Mindfulness Initiative (PMI)
Organizes and supports mindfulness-based meditation and yoga groups in California's prisons and jails.
http://insight-out.org/index.php/programs/mindfulness-in-prison

Bridging Refugee Youth and Children's Services (BRYCS)
A project of the U.S. Conference of Catholic Bishops/Migration and Refugee Services. BRYCS maintains the nation's largest online collection of resources related to refugee and immigrant children and families.
http://www.brycs.org/

The Center for Applied Linguistics' Cultural Orientation Resource Center
This center provides technical assistance regarding the cultural and community orientation refugees receive. http://www.cal.org/what-we-do/projects/cor-center

Centro de Meditación Introspectiva, Redwood City
http://www.insightmeditationcenter.org/espanol/

The National Consortium of Torture Treatment Programs (NCTTP)
A U.S. based network of programs which exists to advance the knowledge, technical capacities and resources devoted to the care of torture survivors living in the United States and acts collectively to prevent torture worldwide.
http://www.ncttp.org/aboutus.html

Web Resources

EthnoMed - Seattle-based Harborview Medical Center's ethnic medicine website contains extensive medical and cultural information about immigrant and refugee groups. Information is specific to groups in the Seattle area, but much of the cultural and health information is of interest and applicable in other geographic areas.
https://ethnomed.org/clinical/mental-health/mental-health

Heal Torture - Resources for practitioners in the mental health field who are serving torture survivors. It provides webinars, evaluator training, publications, links and tools. http://www.healtorture.org/content/mental-health-resources

Chapter 3
Culture, Assessment and Diagnosis

Chapter 3
Culture, Assessment and Diagnosis

What's the use of their having names," the Gnat said, "if they won't answer to them?"
"No use to them," said Alice, "but it's useful to the people that name them, I suppose."

— *Alice in Wonderland* by Lewis Carroll

This chapter provides exercises that enhance our understanding of the variety of ways we express distress and the influence of culture on those expressions. Just as cultures, ethnicities and religions explain and make meaning of symptoms in a variety of ways, so does our "culture" of psychology and counseling. This cautions us to put into context how we name and explain symptoms. Just because we may have our textbooks and even a "bible" of diagnoses, does not mean that we are any less subject to the "consensus trance" in which, psychologist Charles Tart suggests, people believe what they are told to be true as opposed to what they have themselves realized to be true.

ENHANCING ASSESSMENT AND DIAGNOSIS

Practicing the best strategies for assessment and diagnosis, while also considering your client's culture can be a challenge. The following exercises were developed to reduce the challenge and provide a stronger foundation for getting to the appropriate diagnosis.

Diagnosis

The word *hysterical* comes from the word Greek word *hyster* meaning uterus. A woman of ancient Greece felt a terrible pressure rise from her belly, moveup through her diaphragm, and suffocate her speech as it rose to her throat. The diagnosis was hysterike pnix, or the suffocating womb which was believed to have become dislodged. Hence the first diagnosis of what today we call PTSD.

Posttraumatic stress disorder (PTSD) used to be called *hysteria*—a catchall diagnosis. And hysteria is/was not just applied to women. Men used to be described as hysterical in their responses to intensely violent situations and war. The term *shell shock* was coined during World War I since symptoms of hysteria (PTSD) in women seemed similar to the distress experiences of soldiers. During World War I, prominent psychoanalysts suggested that shell shock was only found in "narcissistic, passive, and latently homosexual" men. That diagnosis resulted in men being treated by shipping them back to the battlefront ostensibly to "toughen them up."

Think about modern "consensus trance" diagnostic categories today.

Borderline Personality Disorder: Is borderline our modern hysteria, assigned to "difficult" women and men? Or is it complex traumatic stress in response to sexual abuse?

ADHD: Is it ADHD, or is it chronic stress, poor nutrition and archaic educational systems that operate within a model of sitting still and paying attention for hours on end?

CULTURAL FORMULATION INTERVIEW

Perhaps the best contribution of the DSM-5 is the revised Cultural Formulation Interview (CFI) which has the potential to enhance and ensure an accurate assessment of anyone. It is a set of 16 questions that clinicians may use to obtain information during a mental health assessment about the impact of culture on key aspects of an individual's clinical presentation and care.

Before jumping into the interview, I ask my client questions about their demographics. Depending on the culture and age of the individual I may not obtain all this information in the first meeting. Instead I will wait until we know each other better. Demographic questions may include:

- Place of birth, age, gender, racial/ethnic origin, marital status, family composition, education, language fluencies, sexual orientation, religious or spiritual affiliation, occupation, employment, income
- Migration history, historical or cultural trauma, wars, refugee status, exposure to trauma and torture, dates of migration, migration of family members and who is living in home country.

Following the collection of demographic information, one can choose the basic CFI from the DSM-5 and the optional modules. The objective is to assess cultural factors using a person-centered approach. It allows us to listen to and receive the cultural world view of the client and analyze its contribution to distress.

The CFI also provides an informant version that collects collateral information on the CFI domains from family members or caregivers.

Supplementary modules to the CFI can help clinicians conduct a more comprehensive cultural assessment. The first eight supplementary modules explore the domains of the core CFI in greater depth. The next three modules focus on populations with specific needs, such as children and adolescents, older adults, and immigrants and refugees. The last module explores the experiences and views of individuals who perform caregiving functions.

To prepare for clinical use of the CFI and its modules, practice answering the interview questions and delivering the questions before using it with a client. Pay special attention to the modules that have questions that either you or a client may find challenging or uncomfortable.

CULTURAL TRANSFERENCE AND COUNTERTRANSFERENCE

The traditional psychodynamic concepts of transference and counter transference are valuable when applied to the context of culture and ethnicity. The potential for T/CT is always active in the dyad; when the clinician/client dyad are from different cultures or ethnicities, there is often another level to be explored in order to build trust and deepen the connection.

THERAPIST EXERCISE
CULTURAL FORMULATION INTERVIEW

Directions: Download the core CFI and the supplementary modules from the website listed below. Find a partner at work with whom exchange interviews. Begin first with the core module and progress through each individual module in order to become familiar with the purpose and structure of each one.

- Establish confidentiality and safety for the purpose of mutual learning.

- Consider in your mind something about your belief system, about your health—emotional or physical—that is linked to, or may derive from, your culture, ethnicity, or spirituality/ religion.

- Think about help you receive or seek that you may not always share or feel comfortable discussing.

The CFI interviews are available for use at no charge and may be downloaded on the American Psychiatric Association (APA) website and at: http://www.psychiatry.org/practice/dsm/dsm5/online-assessment-measures#Disorder

THERAPIST WORKSHEET
CULTURAL TRANSFERENCE AND COUNTERTRANSFERENCE

Directions: Please answer the following questions.

Have you experienced *cultural transference* in the clinical setting? Describe what happened?

_____

_____

_____

How did your client express transference?

_____

_____

_____

How did you react initially?

_____

_____

_____

_____

How did you respond?

_____

_____

_____

_____

How might you respond differently today?

_____

_____

_____

_____

Have you experienced _cultural countertransference_ in the clinical setting?

_____

_____

_____

_____

Describe what your client said or did.

_____

_____

_____

_____

How did you react?

_____

_____

_____

_____

How did you respond?

_____

_____

_____

_____

CULTURE AND MEDICINE

The word medicine comes from the Sanskrit word *MA* meaning "to measure." Medicine in its original meaning, attempts to measure or to bring balance to the person, family and community. Since its first use in 13th century English the word has meant art of healing, cure, treatment, remedy, medical art, a potion or plaster. The word also has a similar meaning in other languages such as geneeskunde (Dutch), medizin (German), zÄles (Latvian), ubat (Malay), dawa (Swahili), leigheas (Irish), and medyginiaeth (Welsh).

Our attitudes about medicine, treatment, both receiving and delivering, are informed by our cultural, familial and religious experiences.

Medications & Self-Care

We vary widely in our attitudes toward the use of medications. While generalizations can be made about cultural attitudes, evaluation should always proceed from the specific individual and family. Thus when a client or family expresses their attitudes it may be understood in the context of their cultural milieu.

- African Americans prefer not to be medicated, nor do they trust medication, especially psychotropics.
- Many Latinos feel if they do not receive medications, the clinician has not done their job.

You should collect the following information from your client when discussing attitudes and practices of taking medication:

- List of medications from physicians and non-physicians
- Self-care strategies including herbal medicines, other healers
- Dietary habits (use of nutritional interactions with alternative treatments)
- Individual's/family concept of the illness
- The meaning of the illness in context of culture
- Medication characteristics such as side effects or psychotropic affects which may be important to the patient
- Symbolic power and value of the medication to the client
- Client expectations for medication benefits or risks

THERAPIST WORKSHEET
CULTURAL MEDICINE

I first learned about the use of foods and plants for healing when I lived in western Mexico's jungle where there were no doctors. I relied on the women of the village to help me navigate the numerous subtropical diseases I encountered, along with the accidents, bites, and the many maladies no one could name.

My apprenticeship with the women in the village began very naturally. I learned from trial and error and I served as my own laboratory. It was only later as I sat with my grandmother as she entered her ninth decade that I learned that I came from a long line of Dacian Jewish women who used their hands for healing. These women healed with herbs, foods, and glass cups or wine glasses, to which a little alcohol was added and ignited and then placed flush against their patient's skin. The combustion of the alcohol and evacuation of the oxygen produced a vacuum that would pull up on the skin, creating a suction, which in turn brought blood and oxygen to the surface, dispersing the pain and stagnation in the tissue. This was believed to rid the body of poisons.

The Yiddish saying: *Es vet helfen vi a toiten bahnkes* (It will help like applying cups to a dead person) (Seicol, 1997), points to the centrality and importance of cupping in the healing repertoire of 19th century eastern European Jewish women. "Cupping" is also widely practiced throughout the Middle East, Europe, and by indigenous peoples of the Americas who used a variety of animal horns like buffalo in the old days. Cupping was widely practiced by illustrious Boston physicians through the mid-19th century and it remains an integral method of traditional Chinese medicine, practiced by acupuncturists and massage therapists today.

My great-grandmother brought these traditions with her, along with her borscht, brisket, and the bris (ritual male circumcision) when she left the Old World, but as she and her neighbors settled into their new lives in Boston, cupping and herbs went into the cupboards and they now take their troubles to the *mein tsores* (my troubles) hospital (the Massachusetts General Hospital), where the new medicine was now concerned more with the inside of the body and how chemistry could cure.

Like most immigrants, their diets changed in the new culture along with their physical activity and diseases, setting the stage for the intergenerational epigenetic changes that we continue to see among all immigrants (and native peoples) today.

Have you used any cultural medicines in your practice?

_____

_____

_____

_____

_____

ATTITUDES ABOUT MEDICATION

Directions: Complete this exercise alone or with colleagues.

What are your personal attitudes about psychotropic medications?

_____

_____

What are your attitudes about psychotropic medications for children? Adults?

_____

_____

When you consider a medication referral for a client, what criteria do you consider?

_____

_____

How do you ask your clients how they feel about medication?

_____

_____

Do they feel they require it? Do they believe they will not get well without it?

_____

_____

How do you discuss if they are interested in alternatives to psychotropic medications?

_____

_____

How do you explore your clients' cultural or familial beliefs about medication?

_____

_____

Traditional Medicine

All cultures have traditional medicines. Peoples in every country and every community have a customary system of healing and medicine.

The World Health organization defines traditional medicine as:

> *The sum total of the knowledge, skills, and practices based on the theories, beliefs, and experiences indigenous to different cultures, whether explicable or not, used in the maintenance of health as well as in the prevention, diagnosis, improvement or treatment of physical and mental illness.*

Complementary and Alternative Medicine

Many complementary and alternative medicines (CAM) are derived from traditional medicine practices around the globe. In the process, these practices have been "secularized" (meaning much of the religious, cultural or spiritual ritual has been removed). CAM practices are used by all ethnic groups in the U.S. What is a traditional medicine practice for Asians, like acupuncture and herbs, may be considered a CAM practice for non-Asians. The ability to access and pay for health care also determines use of CAM and whether CAM is self-administered or sought via a practitioner. Studies show that over 65% of adults in the U.S. use CAM but only 35% tell their clinicians about it, suggesting the importance of exploring these questions with clients.

For example, CAM use by Spanish speakers ranges from 50-90% of the population. This includes practices of *Curanderismo,* a syncretic system of healing that combines prayer, medicinal plants, eggs, floral waters, and spiritual cleansings, massage, and ceremony to bring about internal and external balance. It is for physical, mental, and spiritual well-being.

Harmful or Illegal Practices Associated with
Traditional Cultural Values or Religious Practices

Not all traditional practices however should be supported. For example, female genital cutting is a practice of torture and a violation of women's rights. Other practices involved the senseless and illegal killing of wild animals (rhinos, tigers, elephants) and the trafficking in their parts for their purported use for health--frequently male virility.

These practices may include the use of herbal medicines or foods laced with toxins that people unknowingly ingest. For example grasshoppers, a traditional food source in Mexico, were found to contain high levels of lead and were contributing to high lead levels and learning disabilities in children in California.

TRADITIONAL MEDICINE CULTURAL FORMULATION

Directions: Please answer the following questions.

What is your experience with traditional medicine?

_____

_____

_____

Do you currently use any complementary or alternative medicine methods?

_____

_____

_____

Did you know that acupuncture, acupressure, Ayurveda are traditional medicine methods?

_____

_____

_____

How would you respond to a client if she told you she was using herbal medicine to treat insomnia, anxiety or schizophrenia?

_____

_____

_____

_____

_____

CULTURAL IDIOMS OF DISTRESS

Cultural idioms of distress are ways of expressing distress that may not involve specific symptoms or syndromes, but that provide collective, shared ways of experiencing and talking about personal or social concerns. Understanding variations in cultural idioms allows the clinician to enhance diagnosis and treatment and to avoid diagnostic errors.

Awareness of our assumptions as clinicians and broadening our diagnostic criteria to allow for cultural variety is the key to preventing mistakes.

Seeing Ghosts

I was supervising a clinician who presented a case about two children, 8-year-old twins, who were referred for family therapy with their parents as a result of seeing a cousin drown. The clinician reported that the children seemed very agitated and insisted on the fact they had seen ghosts and could not talk about anything else and also drew images of these ghosts during art therapy. The clinician was preparing to diagnose them as psychotic.

Ghosts are a central part of Mexican cultures both indigenous and post-contact Christian. Seeing ghosts and describing them, especially when they are evil, is a common form of expression of distress, loss and grief.

HOW DO YOU COMMUNICATE DISTRESS?

Directions: Please answer the following questions.

Think back to a recent situation in which you felt stressed, sad, or angry. How would you describe your behavior? How did you express your distress?

_____

_____

_____

_____

Have you ever witnessed a friend or family member experience anger, sadness, or grief in a way that was radically different than how you would have? What did you observe and what was your reaction?

_____

_____

_____

_____

People express distress somatically as well as verbally. How do you express your distress? Do you feel physical pain? Do you use your hands, move your body? Stay still? Do you cry?

_____

_____

_____

_____

How did your parents, other family members, and teachers influence the way you express your distress? Were you taught not to cry or to verbalize your discomfort? Were you told not to complain, to "stop your snivelling"Or, if you did, were you called a _quejumbroso/a?_, (Spanish for complainer) a _kvetch_? (Yiddish for complainer) or a _griper_ (British)?

_____

_____

_____

_____

CULTURAL CONCEPTS OF DISTRESS

Directions: Please answer the following questions.

How does your family of origin express distress emotionally and somatically?

_____

_____

_____

_____

Are these forms related to religion? Ethnicity? If so, where do they originate?

_____

_____

_____

_____

If you have two parents, do they each express distress differently?

_____

_____

_____

_____

Are there forms of distress that you have observed that trigger incredulity? Or have you called it a fictitious disorder?

_____

_____

_____

_____

LIMITED LANGUAGE PROFICIENCY

Language is intimately linked to our diagnosis, our use of medications and the benefits derived from treatment. Language is both verbal and nonverbal and forms the basis for establishing rapport connection understanding and treatment success. Clients with limited English proficiency are at a disadvantage in the health system and suffer more. They are less satisfied with their care, more subject to non-adherence with treatment protocols and less likely to benefit from the treatment they do receive.

Did you know?

- Approximately 18% (60 million) of people in the United States speak a language other than English at home.

- 8% (25 million) have limited English proficiency (LEP)

- People with LEP
    - have higher rates of medication complications
    - often do not have a regular source of health care
    - often do not have access to mental health services
    - are less likely to adhere to treatment

Guidelines for Working With a Client and a Translator

- Trained, professional interpreters lead to improved clinical outcomes.

- They increase the use of, and satisfaction with, services for the person with LEP.

- Use a professional translator.

- Seek resources for a translator. If a professional isn't available someone not involved with the family may be an alternate choice.

- Meet ahead of time with the translator to discuss any special words s/he needs to know or potential concepts of distress that may be discussed.

- The clinician speaks in the first person looking directly at the client.

- Ask that the client interact with the clinician.

Case Vignette: Dora and Alicia

Dora and her sister Alicia came to the clinic for a consultation. Alicia was concerned that Dora was showing mood changes. She had gained a lot of weight recently, was anxious and depressed. Alicia could not understand why her sister seemed to change so suddenly. After a thorough intake I discussed what medications she was taking and the doses. She pulled out two bottles of prednisone. One had been prescribed two weeks earlier by a clinician in the local health clinic. When she didn't notice improvement she went to another emergency day clinic but there were no Spanish-speaking translators during her intake. She was examined and given a prescription for prednisone and began taking that dose in addition to her previous one leading to serious side effects.

What would be your next steps with Dora and Alicia?

_____

_____

_____

_____

_____

_____

_____

_____

_____

_____

_____

_____

_____

_____

THERAPIST EXERCISE
LANGUAGE

Directions: Participate in an event that is held in a language other than what you speak or read; it might be a church service, a lecture, or you might view a foreign language video without subtitles.

- *What can you tell about what you are observing based on action and body language?*

- *How did you feel not understanding the language?*

Experience the Language. Take a professional development trip to another country. Learn the basics of a new language that will serve you in your practice. For example, if you work with a Spanish speaking population, travel to Cuba, Mexico or Central America for a language immersion program. While there, sit in a café surrounded by people who speak a language different than your own. How do you feel? What are the challenges navigating in this culture where you understand little? How does this inform your work and your practice?

GRIEF AND MOURNING ACROSS CULTURE AND RELIGION

People in all cultures and religions experience grief. The way these feelings are experienced and expressed is multifaceted. Each culture and religion has its own customary mourning rituals and practices that influence the expression of grief. The familiarity of carrying out these rituals and customs offers a sense of stability and security during times of chaos and loss.

Personal Differences

Individuals often adapt their cultural and religious values to meet their current needs. As a result, responses to grief within a culture or religion vary from person to person—especially in societies made up of people from a variety of cultural and religious backgrounds. At times, this can lead to a person's experience of grief being at odds with cultural and religious expectations. It is important, therefore, to allow people to mourn in ways that feel most natural, given their current experience and cultural context.

To illustrate how people—within any given culture or religion—process grief differently, Susan A. Berger offers the following typology:

- **Nomads**—those who have not yet resolved their grief and don't often understand how their loss has affected their lives
- **Memorialists**—those who are committed to preserving the memory of their loved ones by creating concrete memorials and rituals to honor them
- **Normalizers**—those who are committed to re-creating a sense of family and community
- **Activists**—those who focus on helping other people who are dealing with the same disease or issues that caused their loved one's death
- **Seekers**—those who adopt religious, philosophical, or spiritual beliefs to create meaning in their lives

Berger emphasizes that a person's worldview can change dramatically after a particular loss—leading to a shift in their sense of mortality, their values and priorities, and the manner in which they "fit" in society. The five ways of grieving, she finds, reflect the choices people make in their efforts to adapt to dramatic life changes.

Birth and Death: Hmong and Mexican Practices

The boundaries between the spirit and human world blur during childbirth. In Hmong practice for example, for the month after woman gives birth it is disrespectful to visit any family's homes other than her husband's, because the accumulated lives of her husband's ancestors hang heavily over her. If she visits another family's household, she risks bringing upon them whatever ill fortunes her husband's ancestors have accumulated. She can only visit the home of her husband's family and the homes of families who do not practice Hmong shamanism.

This is a similar concept found in the practice of cuarentena, or quarantine among rural Mexican Indian women. During the 40 days after giving birth, she keeps her head and legs covered lest evil spirits enter. She abstains from sex, others make her special meals rich in herbal remedies, and she does not leave her house while she bonds with her infant.

GRIEF & MOURNING ACROSS CULTURE & RELIGION

How did your family of origin mourn and grieve loss and death?

_____

_____

_____

_____

_____

_____

_____

How do you practice those rituals today in your life?

_____

_____

_____

_____

_____

_____

_____

Are there rituals from other cultures you have observed that you would like to practice?

_____

_____

_____

_____

_____

_____

_____

EXERCISE
GRIEF & MOURNING ACROSS CULTURE & RELIGION

Directions: Match each identity (culture/religion) on the left with its practice of grieving on the right. Answers can be found below.

1. Ojibwe (American Indian)   A. Believe that by divine design, fathers are responsible for providing the necessities of life and protection for their families. In times of grief, the father often puts in extra hours at work, so that he feels he can contribute to the hospital bills or a funeral.

2. Muslim   B. Believe the body of the dead must be bathed, massaged in oils, dressed in new clothes, and then cremated before the next sunrise.

3. Irish   C. Use 'home going' celebrations to connote the deceased is "going home"—to heaven and glory, and to be with the Lord.

4. Tibetan Buddhist   D. Mourn through a "wake", where the extended community of a loved one goes to the nearest pub to help the family through their difficult day through drinking and distraction. The deceased is fondly remembered and toasted throughout the day.

5. Mormon   E. Mourning ceremonies that include singing and the burning of sacred medicines are extremely important. It is believed that one death takes away from the community so they have to find a way to balance that loss.

6. African American   F. Hold a ceremony on the "49th day," to help the deceased perceive their karma so that when they return they are reborn to help this world, rather than continue in the cycle of birth and death.

7. Hindu   G. Widows are expected to observe a longer mourning period, generally of four months and ten days. Crying and weeping at the time of death, at the funeral, and at the burial are all acceptable forms of expression.

1.E, 2.G, 3.D, 4.F, 5.A, 6.C, 7.B

DOMESTIC VIOLENCE ACROSS CULTURES

Domestic violence is found in all cultures. People of all ages and genders are vulnerable to domestic violence. Although the elements of abuse are universal, a person's cultural background influences how individuals deal with abuse and how the community at large responds to it. Cultural influences can create obstacles when working with clients in a domestic violence situation. Understanding a person's belief systems—that vary within and across identity groups—can be helpful in successfully working with that individual.

Challenges to Changing Circumstances in Diverse Populations

A common problem in providing culturally competent care for domestic abuse survivors is that the client may not recognize that they have undergone "abuse"– at least, not as it is recognized in the United States today. Feminist concepts of empowerment are alien to some cultural norms and the risk of losing family and community support is very high.

Racism and Bigotry

The legacy of racism and bigotry in this country has tremendous influence on perceptions around domestic violence. People of certain cultural/religious backgrounds often hesitate to call law enforcement or become involved with the justice system because of their community's or their personal experiences with the police and judicial system.

Immigration and Refugees

Immigrant and refugee communities have more limited access to resources that are necessary for comprehensive support in transitioning out of domestic violence circumstances, including lack of language proficiency, an inability to demonstrate reliable rental history, transportation, a lack of knowledge of laws protecting them, and a complete loss of financial support in the case of leaving home.

DOMESTIC VIOLENCE ASSUMPTIONS

Directions: Please fill out the worksheet. We all have (unconscious) attitudes about the intersection of culture and domestic violence. This exercise provides a way to explore and transform those beliefs.

Parents who abuse their children come from (identify their background):

_____

When I think about abused children I feel:

_____

When I think about parents who abuse their children, I feel:

_____

People batter their partners because:

_____

People who stay in abusive relationships are:

_____

People from this ethnic background _____ **are more likely to abuse their children.**

(Adapted from exercises developed by Judi Sateren, MS, RN, St. Olaf College, Minnesota)

Exercise
Domestic Violence, Culture & Religion Matching Game

Directions: Match each cultural/religious identity on the left with a specific challenge to addressing domestic violence on the right. Answers can be found below.

1. Latina

A. Domestic violence exists at about the same rate as in the heterosexual community.

2. American Indian

B. Because women of this faith are often stereotyped as abrasive, emasculating, and pampered, they may not evoke sympathy from the public or a court of law.

3. Hmong

C. Women often feel compelled to stay in abusive relationships, as it is believed that they are supposed to obey their husbands. They believe that it is their responsibility to maintain peace in the home.

4. African American

D. Fear of loss of respect of their family and clan is a significant factor. Leaving brings shame to the family. Losing face is a powerful deterrent.

5. LGBT

E. At issue is often the experience of being labeled "illegal" or a migrant; they are rarely afforded the label of refugee, which carries some status as a protected group

6. Muslim

F. The fact that a high number of men from this identity group are incarcerated can impact whether or not women seek help, not wanting to put yet another one in prison at the hands of a racist system.

7. Jewish

G. Leaving the reservation may mean leaving supports and family and possibly ostracism for leaving partner

1.E, 2.G, 3.D, 4.F, 5.A, 6.C, 7.B

SELF-INJURY, SCARIFICATION, TATTOOING

The International Society for the Study of Self-Injury defines self-injury as the deliberate, self-inflicted destruction of body tissue without suicidal intent and for purposes not socially sanctioned. It is essential for cultural competency to understand when self-injury is practiced as a maladaptive coping behavior, for example to relieve anxiety or depression, under peer pressure or in response to chronic trauma in contrast to a socially sanctioned activity. Our next focus area is social sanctioned or culturally based self-injury.

Self-injury is also commonly practiced in association with religion, and coming-of-age and spiritual rituals. An important determinant of the value of rituals is whether they are rooted in conscious choice and have a value to the individual and to the group. The popular use of tattoos and body piercing may be understood as a form of ritual self-injury enacted as part of a larger social ritual of becoming and belonging. We are continuously asked to examine our own conditioning and beliefs about these acts.

Some obvious methods of socially condoned (by some) injury include self-flagellation in certain sects of Christianity and male circumcision among Jews and Muslims. Aboriginal cultures in Australia condone women cutting themselves to express their grief.

The Sun Dance has long been a religious and purification tradition of the Plains people and, for many, including the Lakota people, involves extended periods of body piercing. This most sacred of rituals occurs during the summer solstice and is a rite of passage signifying both birth and death and the power of the sun. It represents acts of generosity and the giving of that which one controls: one's body.

 What are your attitudes about tattoos, body piercings and other forms of self-injury?

FEMALE GENITAL MUTILATION/CUTTING

Female genital mutilation (FGM), also called female genital cutting, is a harmful traditional practice that involves the removal of part or all of the female genitalia for non-medical reasons. The World Health Organization classified FGM into four types:

Clitoridectomy — partial or total removal of the clitoris and/or the prepuce

Excision — partial or total removal of the clitoris and the labia minora, with or without excision of the labia majora

Infibulation — the most extreme form, the removal of all external genitalia and the stitching together of the two sides of the vulva

Other — all other harmful procedures done to the female genitalia for nonmedical purposes, for example, pricking, piercing, incising, scraping and cauterization

Who is at Risk?

It is estimated that about 500,000 girls and women are either at risk of or have been subject to genital cutting in the U.S., a number that has doubled since 2000. California, New York and Maryland have the most female immigrants and refugees from countries where female genital cutting is prevalent, suggesting that these states may have a very high number of women at risk for FGC. The countries representing the highest rates for immigrants and refugees in the US are: Egypt, Ethiopia, Somalia, Nigeria, Liberia, Sierra Leone, Sudan, Kenya, Eritrea and Guinea.

Conducting the CFI or a cultural/familial genogram may be a useful way to explore approaches for girls at risk for this procedure.

CASE VIGNETTE: NADEGE & ROSE

Nadege and her daughter, Rose, are referred to you by their primary practitioner. Nadege revealed that she was fearful that Rose's father and family would insist on and carry out genitalia mutilation on Rose when she visits them in Togo for the summer.

Nadege does not believe in female genitalia mutilation. She revealed that the excision of the clitoris together with part or all of the labia minora is a common practice in their region (this is known as type 2 FGM). Nadege wants support in figuring out how to keep Rose safe, by keeping her home, perhaps with a summer school.

What are the laws governing FGM in the U.S. and pertaining to U.S. citizens?

_____

_____

What are the laws assigned to U.S. citizens in your state and what are the laws if a citizen goes out of country? (See list of state laws on this book's website)

_____

_____

What resources are available to you as a practitioner to help Nadege and Rose?

_____

_____

What might be a plan of action to carry out in a systematic way to keep Nadege and her daughter Rose safe?

_____

_____

CULTURAL ADAPTATION OF SERVICES

Diagnosis and treatment that is culturally appropriate and beneficial often requires the adaptation of services in clinical practice, and, at the agency level, administratively. With the emphasis on evidence-based clinical services, this is especially important as many cultural models of care are excluded from evidence-based research. This has led to controversies and dissension among culturally informed clinicians who question whether being evidence-based should be the only criterion for treatment. Since many cultural healing approaches are supported by empirical evidence obtained over thousands of years it behooves us to explore ways in which we can both adapt evidence–based approaches and integrate cultural methods that are important for our clients.

Think about the policies for cultural adaptation of services that you have in place at your agency or practice and identify how you will enact the missing pieces.

Does your agency or practice:

- Adjust the delivery of services so that they are congruent with a client's culture?

- Develop and update their overall cultural competence plan that includes community involvement via needs assessment ?

- Conduct regular planning sessions that include diverse representation on the planning committee to carry out relevant changes in services based on a needs assessment planning?

- Reflect the community diversity culturally, socio-economically, and based on gender and sexual orientation?

- Provide multilingual services including brochures, translators and appropriate assessments?

- Is clinician delivery of services informed by ongoing competency trainings and adaptation of methods to the individual or family need?

- Evaluate appropriate evidence-based practices based on:

  - Has research has been done with the particular culture?

  - Are cultural healing practices being enacted currently in the community?

  - Have empirical cultural practices been researched ?

  - Is there collaboration with community based healers and helpers?

You can visit http://www.healthalt.org for examples of programs nationwide that have applied principles of adaptation.

RESOURCES

Access many of these resources online at www.healthalt.org

Books and Publications

McKay, M.M., Lynn, C.J., Bannon, W.M. (2005). Understanding inner city child mental health need and trauma exposure: implications for preparing urban service providers. *American Journal of Orthopsychiatry, 75*, 201-10.

Mullen, R. F. (2010) Holy stigmata, anorexia and self-mutilation: Parallels in pain and imagining. *Journal For The Study Of Religions & Ideologies*, 9(25): 91-110.

Rudolph, B. M., (1985). *Holy Anorexia*. Chicago, Illinois: University of Chicago Press

Tewari, N., & Alvarez, A. N. (2012). *Asian American Psychology: Current Perspectives*. East Sussex, England Psychology Press.

Zhang, D. (2007). Depression and Culture--A Chinese Perspective. *Canadian Journal Of Counselling And Psychotherapy/ Revue Canadienne De Counseling Et De Psychotheraphie,* 29(3). Retrieved August 3, 2014 from journal hosting of University of Calgary, Canada. http://www.synergiescanada.org/journals/synpra/rcc/11

Movies/Videos/Podcast

On Being radio show has a collection of articles and episodes that relate to grief.
http://www.onbeing.org/search/site/grief

Death is Not the End: Fascinating Funeral Traditions from around the Globe
TED talk by Kate Torgovnick May
http://ideas.ted.com/11-fascinating-funeral-traditions-from-around-the-globe/

Homegoings
PBS film by Christina Turner that explores the little known world of African American funerals and funeral homes.
http://www.pbs.org/black-culture/shows/list/african-american-funeral-traditions/

Web Resources

African Women's Health Center
The mission of the AWHC is to holistically improve the health of refugee and immigrant women who have undergone female genital cutting. It provides access, understanding and community to women who have long-term complications from this tradition and who seek reproductive health care.
http://www.brighamandwomens.org/Departments_and_Services/obgyn/services/africanwomenscenter/default.aspx

Cultural Formulation Interviews (CFI)
The CFI interviews are available for use at no charge with clients/patients and may be downloaded on the American Psychiatric Association (APA) website at:
http://www.psychiatry.org/practice/dsm/dsm5/online-assessment-measures#Disorder

Dimensions of Culture
Provides cross-cultural education, publications, and resources for health care professionals.
http://www.dimensionsofculture.com/2010/11/cultural-aspects-of-death-and-dying/

Hmong
Hmong Spirituality Cosmology
https://geriatrics.stanford.edu/ethnomed/hmong/introduction/spirituality.htmlHmong Grieving

Chapter 4
Cultural Communities

EXPLORE YOUR ATTITUDES ABOUT "ETHNICITIES"

Directions: Let's explore our unconscious attitudes about various cultural and ethnic groups. Pick an ethnicity where you know many people, for example, Mexicans, Chinese, or European Americans. Choose several ethnic identities and then review the variations in your responses.

Close your eyes and allow your stream of consciousness to flow.

What are the first words that rise to your awareness when you think of adults or children who identify as

_____

As an example, if you chose Mexican American, now ask yourself the following questions:

Have you worked with clients who identify as *Mexican American*?

_____

_____

_____

_____

_____

If so, describe the experience:

_____

_____

_____

_____

_____

_____

_____

_____

_____

_____

WHAT'S IN A WORD?

"I use the word 'Texican' to describe myself"

— Mexican American mental health practitioner

We know building rapport is essential for retaining clients, and enhancing treatment outcomes. When working with people who have different ethnic identities, we can avoid offending them by using appropriate terms and simultaneously express our awareness about their culture

Do you use the term Latino? Chicano? Hispanic?

What do each of these terms mean? Latino/a, Chicano/a and Hispanic are often used interchangeably, but have different meanings.

Hispanic has its roots in the Spanish colonization of Central and South America. "Hispania" was the word once used to describe areas conquered by the Spanish. Currently, Hispanic is used to describe someone from a Spanish-speaking country. The US census categorizes people of Central and South American origin as Hispanic.

Latino/a is arguably a more progressive term than Hispanic because it does not connote the loss of identity that occurred during Spanish colonization.

Chicano/a is a term more recently chosen by Mexican Americans to reflect pride is their identity. Like many terms, it is embraced by some and rejected by others, especially more conservative Mexican Americans.

Do you use the term African American? Black? Negro? Colored?

Names change with culture. What we call ourselves and others changes over time. One poll showed that 42% of African Americans preferred to be referred to as black, 35% as African American, and 13% said it didn't matter.

African American is used commonly to refer to descendants of sub-Saharan Africa who were brought to the United States and enslaved. People who have migrated from Africa and naturalize as Americans also use this term.

Negro was a term used more frequently prior to the civil rights movement of the 1960's. It is not commonly used today and its use may be considered offensive.

Referring to individuals as *black* prior to the black power movement, was considered offensive by many. Today it is an acceptable term.

The term *colored* is not used often today because it is associated with Jim Crow laws and discrimination, including signs prohibiting "colored people" from access to businesses or other locales. However, the term people(s) of color is used today, and is considered a preferable term over referring to people as non-white, or minority.

Do you use the term Asian? Oriental?

The term *Asian* is more widely used and accepted than *Oriental* because it does not connote the East versus West identity dualism that carries the connotation of dominant/alternative identities.

Do you use the term Native American? American Indian? Indian?

These terms refer to the original or indigenous peoples in the United States of America. Many indigenous peoples referred to this original land as Turtle Island. The term *American Indian, Indian,* or *Native* are the most preferred terms used by Indians. In contrast, non-native peoples often use the term *Native American.*

Do you use the term Middle Eastern? Arab?

The term *Arab* refers to people whose native language is Arabic. However, in modern usage this term is often (mis)applied to all peoples who come from the Arabian Peninsula or many of the Middle East countries in general.

 Ask your client:
How do you refer to yourself?
How do you identity yourself?

HISPANIC AMERICANS/ LATINOS

Latinos is an overarching term used to describe many peoples from Mexico, Central and South America. As of the 2012, the Latino population in the U.S. was 53 million. Latinos are the largest ethnic minority in the U.S.

Mental Health Care and Latino Americans

Latinos have differing mental health needs, based on their educational and economic status and trauma experienced in their home countries. Puerto Rican and Mexican American children and adults, for example, may be at a higher risk than Cuban Americans for mental health problems, given their average lower educational and economic resources. Central Americans may require more mental health services due to historical trauma in their respective countries arising from internal violence.

Recent immigrants of all backgrounds, who are adapting to the United States, are likely to experience a different set of stressors than long-term Latina/Latino residents. Mexican Americans and European Americans have similar rates of psychiatric disorders, however, Mexican Americans born in the U.S. have higher rates than those born in Mexico. First-generation Latino immigrant youth experience a significantly greater number of mental health problems, than whites, especially depression and anxiety (Potochnick & Perreira, 2010).

EUROPEAN AMERICANS

European Americans (also known as Euro-Americans) are Americans of European ancestry. Euro-Americans are included in the group referred to as "white" and constitute about 64% of the population of the U.S. In the United States, approximately 23% of the population identifies as immigrants or descendants from Germany, 15.5% from Ireland, 13% from England, 6% from Italy, 5% from Mexico 4%, from France, and 4% from Poland. At some point during the migration process, or following, each of these ethnicities experienced cultural trauma and discrimination. Many still do and all experience stereotyping.

Frequently, Euro-Americans think "other" people have an ethnicity; other people have a migration history or heritage. People of Euro-American heritage can also explore their indigenous roots.

This workbook suggests that we all have cultural influences that inform who we are and influence our work as clinicians.

Mental Health Care and Euro-Americans

The Euro-American population, also referred to as non-Hispanic whites, represents 64% of the total U.S. population. Male Euro-Americans are often used as the "baseline" against which data on illness and treatment are normed and assessed. Socioeconomic status, rather than cultural heritage, is actually more predictive of mental and physical health. Excluding drug and alcohol abuse, the prevalence of mental illness in the United States is 44 million (18.5%) of all adults. After American Indians, white non-Hispanic individuals have the highest prevalence of mental illness in the United States.

ASIAN AMERICANS

The Asian American experience is very diverse and cannot be generalized even within the same nationality. With over 4.3 billion people, Asia is the earth's largest and most populated continent. Asian and Indonesian Americans include:

- Chinese
- Japanese
- Korean
- Malaysian
- Myanmar (Burmese)
- Vietnamese
- Laotian
- Cambodian
- Thai

> *"Let me tell you all the things you don't want to know. Like how chink comes from the clanking of metal to railroads as the slaves built train tracks for this country to be connected.*
>
> *Like how the zipperhead down the street is called that because of the way our heads split open when struck with assault weapons or how the jeeps ran over and left marks across corpses and someone clever thought that we were only good to unzip.*
>
> *Like how every Asian person being lumped into one culture is systematically making us assimilate into an America we thought was better than our war torn home and it's stripping away our individuality every time you confuse me with some other nationality that I might share similar features to."*
>
> — from *What Kind Of Asian Are You?* by Alex Dang

Asian American individuals may identify with the country they are from, especially to health practitioners, but among themselves they also identify as a particular indigenous people within their given country. Hence it is important to explore more deeply into the layers of individual identities.

For example, in China there are 56 distinct nationalities. In Japan, there are three populations of significance other than Japanese. In Vietnam, the Kinh people are 87% of the population, but there are 53 other non-Kinh societies with a combined population of 13 million people. These groups include the Thai, Tay, Nung, Dao and Hmong.

Mental Health Care and Asian Americans

Asian Americans as a whole are less likely than other ethnicities to experience mental illness. There are exceptions due to specific identities and cultural exposures. For example, Asian American females between the ages of 65 and 84 have the highest suicide rate of any ethnicity. Also, many Hmong refugee survivors of the Vietnam War experienced PTSD, and second generation immigrants are more likely to experience distress associated with discrimination. There is significant stigma associated with mental illness and many community health efforts are designed to reduce stigma and engage families in understanding depression, suicidality and psychosis.

Some general mental health issues associated with Asian heritage include stress associated with the value assigned to achieving success and the pressure associated with the model minority concept. However, what may be a stressor, like family and ethnic identity, also serve as sources of resilience and social support.

AFRICAN AMERICANS

About 13% of the U.S. population, or roughly 42 million people are African American. African Americans refers to both individuals whose ancestors were brought to the United States as part of the slave trade and also individuals who have migrated recently. Their physical and mental health experiences and their experiences as people of color cannot be compared.

Africans migrating to the United States are one of the largest growing populations and they represent a wide diversity of individuals and reasons for migration, ranging from refugees escaping war, to migration for professional advancement. There are over 1.6 million immigrants from Africa living in the U.S., with males in the majority.

There are more than 1,300 distinct cultures in Africa. Here are just a few of the origins of African Americans:

- Somalia
- Tanzania
- Ethiopia
- Egypt
- Ghana
- Central African Republic
- Sudan

- Southern Sudan
- Zaire
- Nigeria
- South Africa
- Uganda
- Jamaica
- Haiti

Mental Health Care and African Americans

African Americans are more likely than other ethnicities to be victims of violence and thus they are vulnerable to PTSD. Mental distress is also highly correlated with poverty which is high among African Americans. 46% of single mothers with children under the age of 18 live in poverty. Significant racial disparities in health care are linked to poor access in both urban and rural communities. The nexus of stress, poverty and poor nutrition lead to inflammatory diseases like depression, high blood pressure, cardiovascular disease and diabetes. These diseases are prevalent among African Americans, making them vulnerable to chronic disabilities. African American women in particular have been hypothesized to age 7.5 years more quickly due to stress and poverty.

Mental health distress is common among migration associated with refugee status and escape from war and torture. Physical and mental illness frequently co-occur and there is often stigma associated with seeking help. This is exacerbated by loss of family as a protective network. Conducting research on the specific cultural experiences of the individual and family is essential to treatment. Furthermore there is often a mismatch between DSM nosology and specific cultural expressions and explanations of distress. While African migrants may have been exposed to extreme stress and discrimination due to their tribal identities in their country of origin, prior to arrival in the U.S., they do not generally have the experience of racism common to African Americans in the United States. Coping with racism and African foreigner privilege, along with all aspects of acculturation may be a focus of support. As the author Mukoma Wa Ngugi suggests: "Racism wears a smile when meeting an African; it glares with hostility when meeting an African American."

AMERICAN INDIANS AND ALASKA NATIVES

The original peoples of North America and the Pacific Islands share common historical experiences with outsider invasions mainly from European kingdoms on the mainland, and from Chinese and Arabic peoples in the islands. For many descendants of indigenous peoples who directly experienced these invasions, the events and their physical, emotional and mental effects are as fresh as if they occurred yesterday. Meanwhile, many people continue to experience marginalization, and removal from homelands, creating significant social, emotional, physical and mental dislocation. These peoples are referred to commonly as:

- Alaskan Native (more than 200 communities and nations)
- American Indian (more the 550 communities and nations)
- First Nations (Canada) (more than 500 bands and communities)
- Native Hawaiian (Hawaiian)
- Other Pacific Islander (Guam, Samoa)

Mental Health Care and American Indians and Alaskan Natives

More than 4 million Americans identify as American Indians and Alaskan Natives. More than two-thirds of all native people live in urban environments, not on reservations. There is extraordinary cultural and socioeconomic diversity among native peoples in the U.S., but overall higher rates of poverty when compared to other ethnicities in the U.S.

Generally, the mental health of people on reservations is worse than that off the reservations. The major mental health issues affecting native peoples include depression, substance abuse, and posttraumatic stress disorder. There are also high rates of physical disability due to accidents, injuries and chronic physical problems like diabetes, that also intersect with mental health.

There are special issues associated with native status, in particular, historical and intergenerational trauma. This includes the ongoing effects of colonization, loss of land, and loss of natural resources. Trauma still exists from the boarding school experience in the late 19th and early 20th centuries where American Indian children were forcibly removed from their homes to attend schools where their language and customs were banned. Abuse was widespread and American Indian children were removed from their homes to non-American Indian foster care homes.

Culture-based interventions are used widely for treatment mental and physical health often alongside evidence-based interventions.

EASTERN MEDITERRANEAN AMERICAN AND ARAB AMERICANS

Peoples located in the eastern Mediterranean region can be different from one another culturally, linguistically, and socially. Despite these differences, when peoples from different countries such as Bahrain, Kuwait, Syria, or Saudi Arabia emigrate to the United States they nearly always become classified as Arab. Not only is this misleading, but to place all peoples in the "Arabic" basket is to dismiss or demean, the rich cultural heritage each person represents.

The many cultures in the Eastern Mediterranean region demand that clinicians familiarize themselves with the rich diversity of the peoples so as to better serve client needs. Here are some of the peoples located in the Eastern

Mediterranean region and along the northeastern African coast where Eastern Mediterranean influences have evolved over the last seven hundred years.

• Bahraini	• Yemeni	• Saudi Arabian
• Palestinian	• Iraqi	• Tunisian
• Bedouin	• Somali	• Syrian
• Assyrian	• Sudanese	• Lebanese
• Kuwaiti	• Libyan	• Armenian

Mental Health Care, Eastern Mediterranean Americans and Arab Americans

There is significant cultural and religious diversity among Eastern Mediterranean Americans and Arab Americans. There is also a cultural mistrust of mental health, alongside stigma associated with seeking mental health services. The majority of Eastern Mediterranean people in the United States are Christian, and not Muslim. However since 9/11 there has been a substantial increase in hate crimes and overall discrimination against people who "appear" to be of Eastern Mediterranean or Arabic origin. This has contributed to stress, depression and may also exacerbate domestic violence.

Among recent migrants from the Middle East, similar to all migrants and refugees, depression, PTSD, anxiety and interpersonal partner violence are major concerns. The need for bicultural and bilingual clinicians is important. The influence of generational status, religion and the role of the "social net" as well as reduction of isolation in the lives of clients is the foundation for culturally sensitive work.

PACIFIC ISLANDERS

One and a quarter million people (0.4% of the population) in the United States identify as Native Hawaiian and other Pacific Islander, either alone or in combination with other communities. Over 56% of the Native Hawaiian and other Pacific Islander population report multiple cultural heritages.

Pacific Islanders are peoples of the Pacific Island region that includes:

- Polynesia (Hawaii, the Easter Islands, and New Zealand)
- Melanesia (Fiji, Papua New Guinea, Solomon Islands, Vanuatu Islands, and New Caledonia)
- Micronesia (eight territories including Guam, Kiribati, and the Marshall Islands)

Mental Health Care and Pacific Islanders

Most Pacific Islanders are indigenous to their lands and descendants of the original inhabitants of land claimed by the United States. There is great diversity in this wide-ranging geographic population. The stress of colonization and cultural trauma include loss of land, changes in diet and traditional practices. This is reflected in higher levels of accidents, and chronic illnesses like diabetes, cardiovascular disease and cancer. Some of the extremely high rates of cancers are associated with nuclear testing in these territories in the 1950's. Similar to the mental health challenges found among American Indians and Alaskan Natives, Native Hawaiian youth are at a higher risk for depression and suicide.

Yet there is ongoing resilience in the face of the effects of cultural stress. Hawaii, like all the territories, has a rich heritage of traditional rituals and healing methods and there is a strong cultural and traditional medicine revitalization movement for both restoration of health through traditional foods and support of cultural values of holism and balance, family and compassion. Traditional methods of healing include the use of massage, medicinal plants, prayer, ritual, and Ho'oponopono, a method of resolve conflicts.

SKIN COLOR

The whole question of referring to people by color is fraught with illusion. While we often use color as an identifier, just as "race" is used, personally, professionally, and in the media, it tells us little about who people actually are and is most often misleading.

Colorism is the assignment of status based on one's skin color. Color is used to discriminate, while many cultures privilege lighter color skin, others consider it "evil."

The whole concept of "passing" is based in part on skin color. In the U.S., the lighter one's skin color, the more benefits it confers among some groups. Research shows lighter skinned African Americans are regarded more positively by many people and are considered more beautiful. American Indians who are lighter skinned are treated better, and many Asian Americans also adhere to a "lighter is better" belief. This attitude also exists in many African and Asian countries. Ironically, many white-skinned people often show status by tanning.

Consider Skin Color in Your Identity
What are the terms used to describe who you are, based on the color of your skin?

CULTURAL TRAUMA AND HISTORICAL TRAUMA

Cultural trauma, historical trauma, and intergenerational trauma are among the concepts used to explain the response to chronic stress among whole groups of people and how this stress is "transferred" across generations. These terms derive from observations that cultural groups who are exposed to prolonged stress and suffering from war, genocide, and interpersonal violence initiates the transfer of psychological and physical stress to offspring and subsequent generations. It is often associated with learned helplessness and depression.

Research has been conducted among survivors of the Nazi Holocaust, the Khmer of Cambodia, American Indians, and aboriginal peoples of North America and Mexico and Australia. The concept of unresolved grief is also central to large community losses sustained over decades or centuries.

Cultural trauma and historical trauma in the life of the client should be explored as part of the assessment process in order to gain a full understanding of the influences and meaning of family well-being. Often people do not share this information, unless asked. It may be considered private, invisible, or not considered, especially among clinicians of a different ethnicity.

Here are a few examples of cultural and historical trauma in the United States

Japanese Americans

Many Asian families have, together or separately, navigated out of perilous situations across the ocean as "boat people." There are large numbers of refugees from Asian countries, many of whom are economic refugees, escaping from the tumult of war and reckless development. For many however, the traumas and losses occurred generations after arrival in the United States. For example, the Japanese American internment camps during World War II, when over 100,000 Japanese people were forcibly relocated in concentration camps in connection with the attack on Pearl Harbor. The consequences of internment not only devastated the lives of all internees but undermined the Issei's (the first generation's) cultural foundations. These first generation fathers experienced depression, social identity crisis, and an extreme sense of helplessness. The fissure between parents and children widened as the younger generation faced the constant pressure to Americanize. By the end of the war in 1945, Japanese Americans had lost family savings, homes, farms, and businesses they had prior to the war. Then in their 60s, the first generation had no economic legacies or family trades to pass on to their children. They were forced to start from scratch, seeking employment in manual labor, while their children struggled to merge into the mainstream.

African Americans

In United States, the legacy of slavery is a cultural wound that remains unresolved and unhealed and has resulted in among other symptoms, the mass incarceration of African American men and women.

Irish Americans and American Indians

At first glance, one would not think to make connections between cultural trauma among the Irish and American Indians. Yet there are ways in which these diverse cultural groups share very similar experiences. For centuries the Irish lived as a conquered people in their own land. Great Britain controlled the politics, economics and religious life of Ireland. Subjugation and conflict gave rise to an unmistakable Irish identity and a sense of cohesion even amidst the "troubles," the trauma. Frank McCourt, the author of *Angela's Ashes*, sums it up when he writes:

> *"When I look back on my childhood I wonder how I survived at all. It was, of course, a miserable childhood: the happy childhood is hardly worth your while. Worse than the ordinary miserable childhood is the miserable Irish childhood, and worse yet is the miserable Irish Catholic childhood . . . nothing can compare with the Irish version: the poverty; the shiftless loquacious alcoholic father; the pious defeated mother moaning by the fire; pompous priests; bullying schoolmasters; the English and the terrible things they did to us for 800 long years."*

The Irish experience has been compared to the American Indian experience of colonization. Indeed the British "practiced" their colonization techniques on the Irish, administering policies from London through the Bureau of Irish Affairs. Later, the United States practiced similar policies through the Bureau of Indian Affairs. Similarities include the role of substance abuse as self-medication (over 50% of the Irish state they abuse alcohol compared to under 30% in other European countries), a sense of shame, poor self-esteem, a sense of inferiority and high levels of (domestic) violence.

Colonization by the British and extraction of resources, the "Great Hunger" (caused by potato blight and British policies which hurt the poor), and extensive sexual and physical abuse by clergy are a few of the contributing factors of multigenerational trauma that affect the Irish. This trauma is carried by Irish Americans in cellular memory.

The traditions of cultural revitalization similar to those carried out by American Indian communities are also underway in Ireland. The learning of Irish language, restoration of traditional foods and song are part of a global effort among indigenous peoples to reclaim sobriety and self-care in the aftermath of generations of trauma and genocide.

Irish Indians

I went to Ireland with my colleagues from the Center for World Indigenous Studies to co-host a conference on violence and coexistence. One afternoon, a group of us were walking through a public square in Dublin when a very old man came up slowly and grabbed the hand of Russell Jim, the Director of Environmental Restoration from Nuclear Waste on Yakama Indian land. "Thank-you, thank-you sir," the old man said. Russell replied, "Well you are very welcome, but why are you thanking me?" The old man said, "your people saved mine during the potato famine. We were starving and your people sent us food. We starved because the English took our food, just like they took yours. But you saved us. We are the Irish Indians."

THE HISTORICAL LOSS SCALE (HLS)

The assessment of Historical trauma may be used with individuals and whole communities to explore the effect of community trauma on the lives of individuals.

The HLS is a 12-item measure developed to measure how often thoughts pertaining to historical loss occur. Some examples of the types of historical losses included in this instrument are loss of land, language, culture, and traditional spiritual ways as well as loss of family/family ties.

The Historical Loss-Associated Symptoms Scale

The HLASS is a 17-item measure of the frequency with which certain emotions are experienced in thinking about, or being reminded of, historical losses among Indian people and culture.

Explore your observations or experience as a clinician as you consider the role of unresolved cultural trauma in the ongoing cultural and interpersonal traumas affecting people of color in the United States.

Cultural Distress Symptoms/Syndromes

Directions: Review cultural expressions of distress from around the globe. Match each culture-bound syndrome on the left with its description on the right.

1. Amok (Amuk or Amuck)

A. First identified in West Africa. Affects youths under high pressure to succeed. Difficulty with concentration and cognitive abilities, sleep problems, headaches, eye and neck pain, and other somatic complaints.

2. Anorexia Mirabilis (Holy Anorexia)

B. Originates in Taiwan. An individual who becomes possessed by an ancestor of their family. Symptoms include visual and auditory hallucinations and confusion. May be related to stress regarding family, and many sufferers of the illness are women. Treatment can be found in therapy, medication, or meditation.

3. Anorexia Nervosa

C. Occurs among African Americans in southern U.S. and in Caribbean groups. Includes a sudden collapse and fainting without warning with inability to move or see with eyes open, dizziness, and sudden weakness of the body. Occurs in response to funerals, shocking news, and stressful school situations.

4. Boufee Deliriante

D. Affects, but not limited to, people of North America and Europe. The restriction of caloric intake in order to lose weight or maintain a certain weight. The individual must be below the average weight for their height and weight. Many factors contribute to the development of anorexia nervosa such as family history, body image, nutritional deficits and media influence.

5. Brain Fag

E. Similar to startle disorder or as a result from shock and often includes dancing or wildly gesticulating, screaming or laughter. Found in Indonesia and Malaysia.

6. Bulimia Nervosa

F. Occurs in Miskitu Indians, Nicaragua. Spirit possession; person becomes very violent and experiences seizures, loss of speech, and altered consciousness. Treatable by a healer with herbs. May affect groups of people that are generally in close contact.

7. Dhat

G. Occurs in China. Symptoms of dizziness, loss of appetite, insomnia, and anxiety. Many symptoms are non-specific and affect the body as well as the mind. Treatment includes traditional Chinese herbal medicine or counseling. Also known as stress or a nervous breakdown. It is often used as a diagnosis to avoid the stigma of mental illness.

8. Falling Out

H. Affects mostly Malay and Indonesian people (males). Signs of depression or detachment leading to violent outbursts that may result in homicide. Believed to be caused by an evil spirit entering the body.

9. Grisi Siknis

I. Found in Malaysia, South Asia, East Asia, and Europe. An individual believes that their penis is being retracted into their body, leading to short-term suffering, although no damage to the genitals occurs. Rarely, a woman will believe her nipples or vulva are retracting into her body. May also experience shortness of breath, dizziness, and other symptoms. Treatments in Asia include prayer, herbal medicine, and animal penis.

10. Hwa-byung or Wool-hwa-byung

J. An intense fear of embarrassing oneself in front of another due to their body odor, appearance, or facial expressions. Extreme social anxiety or heightened self-consciousness. Occurs primarily in Japan and Korea but is not limited to these regions.

11. Hsieh-ping

K. Reactive depression or extreme sadness following the break up or loss of a partner. Symptoms include anorexia, insomnia, feelings of worthlessness, and anger. Especially found in Trinidad.

12. Koro / Shrinking Penis / Genital Retraction Syndrome

L. Sudden outburst of aggression; involves hallucinations, marked confusion, psychomotor agitation, and paranoia. Found in West Africa, Haiti, and Canada.

13. Latah

M. An individual eats large amounts of food followed by a purging; could include vomiting, exercising, and diuretics. Females are affected more often. Nutritional deficits, poor body image, obesity, and anxiety may cause an increased risk of developing bulimia nervosa. Occurs in North America and Europe.

14. Pibloktoq

N. Found predominantly in Korea and translates to fire-illness. Symptoms include anger, depression, anxiety, and distorted thinking. Middle-aged women are the largest group of individuals affected. The stress of family and daily life are examples of a few stressors that could cause hwa-byung. Treatment may include therapy or religious practices and meditation therapy.

15. Qigong deviation or Kundalini Psychosis

O. Restriction of food intake in order to cleanse spiritually and religiously. First observed in medieval times by women sacrificing their bodies to perfect their relationship with God.

16. Shenjian Shuariuo / Neurasthenia / Americanitis

P. Found in China and around the world. Excessive meditation, or medication in people developmentally unprepared for the powerful surge of energy that increases awareness may lead to qigong or Kundalini psychosis. Is considered a result from uncontrolled flow of chi or energy. Treatment includes cessation of meditation activities, massage, acupuncture, and counseling.

17. Tabanka

Q. Arctic hysteria is an illness that occurs around the Arctic circle among the Inuit people. Includes dissociative behaviors, psychosis, withdrawal, anxiety, and suicide. Occurs more often in winter and it may be associated with lack of sun exposure. Women are affected by it more often than men. There is controversy around the actual existence of this syndrome.

18. Taijin Kyofusho

R. Usually women possessed by demons, though among people who have migrated it is more often men. Ethiopian Christians and Muslims believe it is the cause of mental illness. Found in North Africa and the Middle East.

19. Zār

S. Primarily found in India, though also in Spain and Russia. Symptoms include anxiety, depression, decreased libido, impotence, and distorted perception of penis.

CULTURAL NAME OF ILLNESS

I want to know what my client calls their illness, how they explain it, and how they treat it.

I want to identify how we can coordinate treatment together and how I might enhance their approach, or if it is dangerous gently offer some alternatives. **Like you, I don't want to accidentally offend my client, so I have developed a way of explaining to my clients why I am asking certain questions:**

- *"Often times we grow up in our families/communities with a variety of names for our distress or discomfort. Yet, sometimes when we move locations, health professionals are not familiar with these terms. This then can lead us to keep them to ourselves. However, I'm very interested to hear about your experiences and hear the names you would give to your symptoms. This would help me help you better."*

- *Can you share with me what you call what you are experiencing?*

- *Have you had an experience where you have tried to share this information with a professional and felt unheard?*

- *What traditional methods have you used to resolve these issues?*

- *Have they helped or helped in part, or not at all?*

- *Sometimes we can combine other methods along with the methods you describe to enhance their effectiveness. Are you interested in exploring this?*

Sobador

When I worked in the jungle there were several sobadors (bonesetter) who used various liniments(liquids rubbed on the body to relieve pain) while giving a massage to heal sprains. Among the liniments used were herbal liniments infused with chamomile, rosemary and, mota (cannabis). One day a woman came to the clinic with burns on her arm. She had seen one of the sobadores who used a liniment made of petroleum (gasoline). She had gone to see him for an arm sprain but the petroleo was not a good base for the lotion. I went to visit the sobador, whom I knew, to discuss his methods and had to sensitively navigate a discussion about how petroleo could cause problems with some people, that it could burn and was likely not the best base to use. I asked him about his other lotions and was very effusive in my interest and support of these other liniments, suggesting that I felt they were likely even more beneficial than the petroleum and they had the added benefit of not burning the client. I also had some oils that I offered to give him and every so often would send some oils over for him to use to reduce the burden of his finding good quality oils. We developed a good working relationship and referred clients to each other.

Once we know how a client thinks about his or her symptoms or illness we also explore what they have done to address it. I am especially interested in how their treatment interventions are either used at home, or whether they have visited a healer or another type of clinician.

Traditional cultural belief systems usually have corollaries in cultural constructs of treatment systems. Thus the next exploration is a cultural belief system called *curanderismo*, a commonly practiced approach to health and healing in the United States, Mexico and Central America.

What is Curanderismo?

Curanderismo is a form of traditional medicine that is syncretic. It combines indigenous practices of Mexico with medical practices brought over by settlers from Europe. It approaches wellness as holistic; disease is not solely rooted in the physical but also derives from spiritual and mental causes.

In the United States, *curanderismo* is most commonly used to complement the traditional biomedical system, however often people will visit a *curandero/a* before visiting a biomedical professional. *Curanderos* use a wide range of objects in their work, including:

- Herbs, Plants, Eggs
- Limes
- Prayer, Massage, Chanting
- Holy Water
- Incense
- Oils and candles

Each *curandero* has a unique practice and may incorporate different objects and prayers into their rituals. For example, one *curandero* may perform a spiritual cleansing, or *limpia*, with a raw unbroken egg while another may utilize a bundle of herbs as a cleansing tool. Eggs are used to absorb the bad spirit/energies of the patient, which are then destroyed when the egg is broken.

Watch the following YouTube clip for an example of a limpia cleansing:
http://www.youtube.com/watch?v=SoJUzuu0BF4&index=2&list=PLB9273958A6A4F642

Listen to an explanation of a curandero working in Fresno California:
http://www.youtube.com/watch?v=q7WCD0nMMlU

Creating an Offering as Healing Ritual with a Client

The rituals of prayer, offering gifts to the gods and goddesses, requests for protection and healing and remembering loved ones, the past, and planning and hoping for the future all come together in the creation of offerings placed on altars. Altars are found across all cultures in a variety of designs and purposes. Altars may be found in formal places of worship as well as made at home or work. Home altars are created by both Latino and Haitian families and are central to healing and spiritual practices. We observe offerings on Buddhist altars upon walking in to a Vietnamese grocery store. We observe, but rarely add to, the formal altars in churches and temples of worship. Offerings however vary widely by religion and belief system. *Offrandes* among Haitians are typically made weekly on Saturday and Sunday during a *divine service*, though a client can create an altar any time of year.

Offerings need not be enacted as part of a specific religion per se but may be used as a way for your client to gather objects s/he considers important and used to focus and meditate and as a way to discuss through the artistic representation and placement of objects, feelings that may be difficult to verbalize. Thus an offering upon an altar can become a form of art therapy infused with a deep meaning that finds layered expression.

In my office I have co-created altars with clients who expressed an interest and need to grieve, worship or focus their intention. We do this by creating "the offering" called *ofrenda* in Spanish, *offrande* (Haitian-French) which consists of objects of importance and meaning that are gathered and placed at the altar. I serve as a supportive facilitator.

Next is an example of a process of making an *ofrenda* I have done with clients who are grieving. Keep in mind you can be creative in making the *ofrenda*. Creating an "offering" may not be appropriate for your client or may not be appropriate to do in your office.

EXERCISE

OFRENDA

Directions: An *ofrenda* may include a collection of images, objects, and foods that are placed on an altar during the Dia de los Muertos celebration, which is celebrated in Mexico and many other Latin American countries. *Ofrendas* are commonly created in order to remember and honor deceased loved ones. This exercise will show you how to help a client construct his or her own *ofrenda* as an opportunity to grieve in a culturally congruent manner and to share this process with you as the therapist. Explain to the client that they can make the *ofrenda* at home or in your office. If they make the *ofrenda* at home, ask them to take a photograph to show you. This exercise is intended for a client of any culture or background.

Alternative Exercise: A similar, though more secular, art based project is to create a cultural memory box as a method of exploring memories and feelings.

BENEFITS OF THIS EXERCISE

Constructing an *ofrenda* allows for a non-confrontational conversation about death and grief. *Ofrenda*-making also adds in feelings of appreciation and love to the grieving process.

When: While *ofrendas* are typically made each year on November 2nd during Dia de los Muertos, your client can create an altar any time of year.

Who: This exercise can also be used with children, with the supervision of a parent or other adult.

Materials:

- Small table
- Tablecloth or fabric
- Traditional elements (include any or all):
- Candles (1 for each person being honored)
- Glass of water
- Incense
- Marigolds or other brightly colored flowers (fresh, dried, or paper)
- Favorite foods of the deceased
- Framed photograph of the person being honored
- Personal items of the deceased (jewelry, watch, handkerchief, etc.)
- Sugar skulls or other decorative items
- Ceramics and woven baskets

Instructions:

1. Find the proper location for the *ofrenda*- a small table pushed against a wall is ideal. Cover the table with a piece of fabric or cloth.
2. Place photographs of the deceased in the center of the table. Make sure that each person being honored has a candle.
3. Place personal items of the deceased (jewelry, watch, etc.) on the table. Add candles, incense and incense holder, flowers, foods, glass of water in the front and center of the table.

Next Steps:

You may use the different items on the *ofrenda* to ask questions.

Tell me about your grandmother?

Tell me about this item and what it means to you?

What did it mean to your grandmother?

Are these some foods that she loved?

Tell me about a time you recall enjoying a meal with her? Or a party?

CULTURAL MEMORY BOX

Sometimes expressing feelings is easier through art than words. In this exercise, you will help a client create a cultural memory box to explore feelings of grief, loss, and remembrance of loved ones. This exercise can also be used with a client who has emigrated as a way of reconnecting with the family they left behind. This exercise is appropriate for a client of any age. See note below on using this exercise with children.

Directions:

1. Have your client decorate the outside of his or her memory box using images cut from old magazines, books, etc. Explain that they can decorate the box in any way that appeals to them. Images can be of people, things, or places from the client's memory.
2. Ask your client to place mementos and objects of symbolic meaning in their memory box. These can be of a loved one who has passed on, a friendship that has ended, or of the client's homeland. In this way, the box marks an important transition.
3. Add to this cultural memory box; encourage your client to add objects to their box as they wish.

Materials:

- Cardboard or wooden box, of any shape and size

- Old magazines

- Collected mementos, including:

- Photos or drawings of loved ones/home

- Tokens

- Buttons, figurines, dolls, matchboxes, jewelry, or other objects of symbolic meaning.

- Markers, colored pencils, pens, and crayons

- Scissors

- Glue-stick, Mod-podge, or other craft clue

- Ribbons, stickers, or other decorative items

NOTE: This exercise can be modified to use with children ages six to 17. It may be useful to work together with the child to select images and objects that are significant to him or her. Ask "What words would you use to describe [loved one/homeland]" and draw their responses onto the box. Ask the child to remember sensory details of their memory; the way their home smelled, the softness of a pet's fur, etc. Using these details, help them choose objects that evoke these memories.

HEALING METHODS

Directions: During a cultural formulation interview or assessment as you are getting to know a client, it is useful to ask the following question when you wish to explore their cultural or alternative forms of healing.

"Often, people look for help from many different sources, including different kinds of doctors, helpers, or healers. In the past, what kinds of treatment, help, advice, or healing have you sought for your [Insert: the problem they named previously]?"

"I know that curanderismo is widely used in your culture. I think it's a very interesting form of healing. I know that many people with your symptoms seek out a curandero/a and often benefit from their treatment. Is this something you have done or might consider?"

This informs my client that s/he may feel safe in sharing the methods she is exploring for treatment and it opens the dialogue.

- *Have you used this form of healing?*

- *If so, can you tell me about it?*

- *How has it helped you?*

- *Are there areas where you feel I can be of support your health and healing process?*

Questions to ascertain use of herbs or other medication:

- *I know that in your culture, like mine, herbs are commonly used for physical and emotional stress. I think herbs can be very helpful for a variety of reasons.*

- *Are you currently using any?*

- *If so, which ones?*

- *I want to make sure that the herbs you are using will work well with the medications you are also using so that we ensure your safety and benefits of both."*

CULTURAL HEALING ATTITUDES EXERCISE

Directions: This exercise may be adapted to any exploration of attitudes about cultural healing methods. Feel free to insert topics and replace the word "*curanderismo*" with other methods, for example Vodou, sweat lodge, peyote ceremony, Christian Science Prayer, Reiki etc.

Write five words that describe your initial response to *curanderismo*:

1. _____

2. _____

3. _____

4. _____

5. _____

Would you have any obstacles in collaborating with or referring to a curandero/a? Why or why not?

_____

_____

_____

_____

_____

If you had negative responses, can you explore what you might need to change those responses into positive ones? Is that possible? Or does your belief systems prevent that?

_____

_____

_____

_____

_____

_____

THE MEANING OF MATERIAL WEALTH EXERCISE

Cultural memories may include mementos and objects that have meaning. They may also include beliefs about money and material culture that have been handed down from one generation to the next. We carry those beliefs and often act on them or react to them.

Directions: Explore the beliefs you carry about material wealth and where they come from.

What did/does money mean to your grandparents?

_____

_____

_____

_____

_____

What did they spend their money on? How do/did they save money?

_____

_____

_____

_____

Aside from money, what kind of objects or other materials were most valuable to them?

_____

_____

_____

_____

_____

In what ways were/are your grandparents resourceful? Your parents?

_____

_____

_____

_____

_____

_____

What kind of objects or other materials were most valuable to them?

_____

_____

_____

_____

_____

_____

What did you learn from your parents/grandparents about being resourceful?

_____

_____

_____

_____

_____

_____

TRADITIONAL CLOTHING

Cultural differences are emblematic in clothing: what we wear is a reflection of the nature of our social and natural environment—mirroring its challenges and pleasures. Like an actor metamorphosing into a character, dancers from traditional cultures disappearing behind masks, athletes equipping themselves in their gear, and hunters melding into the forest, costume is a way of participating with your environment through appearance.

In many cultures, there are various kinds of pressure on men and women to dress certain ways.

Directions: Please complete the worksheet.

What kinds of pressures do you feel to dress a certain way?

_____

_____

_____

Name some ways in which you make decisions or judgments about people based on how they dress.

_____

_____

_____

Why do you believe or feel the way you do?

_____

_____

_____

When you travel in the U.S. or to other countries what do you observe about dress? How do you react?

_____

_____

_____

As gender expression becomes more fluid in the U.S. and other countries, the pressure to dress according to a standard defined by sex and gender also becomes blurred. Men are wearing skirts and blouses or dresses, women letting their moustaches grow...

How do you feel when you see gender-bending dress?

_____

_____

_____

How might you expand the spectrum of your dress mode?

_____

_____

_____

LANGUAGE

As I explored in Chapter 2, language can be an obstacle to understanding when the client and clinician speak different languages. Language also is limited if the clinician lacks awareness of the historical migration experience of the client and observes a client's hesitation to discuss painful experiences.

Juana

Juana presents speaking some Spanish and another language which you do not recognize. She said that her first language is Tzotzil. You ask a translator to join you who was skilled in Tzotzil and Spanish. Juana discussed the trauma of migration and relocation and some health problems at your first meeting. She spoke of losing her sister and brother during an event involving the military, but she did not want to discuss it any further. She said she hasn't slept well since this event.

Follow-up response:

"Juana I was very moved by your story and what you shared with me about your history. I am very interested to know more about your experiences and so I took the liberty to learn a little bit about the Tzotzil language and the Mayan Indians who speak it. Of course I would be very honored if you would share with me a little bit about your cultural heritage. I know that there are 7 groups that speak Tzotzil. Do you belong to any of these groups?

I also learned that in 1977 there were massacres by the military. I know that this is painful for you to talk about and you don't need to until you are ready. I can only imagine what a terrible experience this was and I want you to know that if you wish to share I am going to be present and listening."

Marie

Marie presented speaking some Creole and another language, which you do not recognize. She said that her first language is Creole. You asked a translator to join you who was skilled in Creole. Marie discussed the trauma of migration and relocation and some health problems at your first meeting. She spoke of losing her sister and brother during an event involving natural disaster, but she did not want to discuss it any further. She said she hasn't slept well since this event.

Follow-up response:

"Marie I was very moved by your story and what you shared with me about your history. I am very interested to know more about your experiences and so I took the liberty to learn a little bit about the Creole language and French. Of course I would be very honored if you would share with me a little bit about your cultural heritage. I know that there is a majority that speak Creole, and French… Do you belong to any of these groups?

I also learned that in 2010 there was a terrible earthquake. I know that this is painful for you to talk about and you don't need to until you are ready. I can only imagine what a terrible experience this was and I want you to know that if you wish to share I am going to be present and listening."

MULTI-LINGUAL FAMILIES

Directions: Please answer the following questions.

Do any of your family members speak a different language than you? If so, name the language(s):

_____

_____

_____

_____

Does your mother speak your father's language—and vice versa?

_____

_____

_____

_____

Be mindful of the greater social pressure of women to keep traditions alive by "maternal tongue."

Was one of your parents' cultures a "dominant" ancestry (English, French, Spanish) in contrast to a "minority" ethnicity?

_____

_____

_____

_____

Were you raised to feel respect and pride towards your multicultural lineage—both to the dominant and minority cultures of your parents?

_____

_____

_____

_____

Did you ever feel that one of your parents expressed racism toward their spouse?

_____

_____

_____

Do/did you feel accepted by your grandparents?

_____

_____

_____

Have you been encouraged to learn other languages by your family?

_____

_____

_____

Do you think that you would feel closer to these members if you spoke their language?

_____

_____

_____

What strategies do you use (or might you consider) to build relationships to family members/ friends who you can't talk with?

_____

_____

_____

_____

LANGUAGES IN YOUR FAMILY EXERCISE

Directions: Please complete the following worksheet.

Make a list of the spoken languages shared (or not shared) in your family.

_____

_____

_____

_____

_____

Make a list of the non-verbal expressive outlets (hobbies) shared (or not shared) in your family. They might include: fishing, playing a musical instrument, creative arts, cooking, woodworking, etc.

_____

_____

_____

_____

_____

Describe the dominant verbal and non-verbal modes of "language" in your family?

_____

_____

_____

_____

_____

Addressing Stereotypes

All cultural communities are subjected to constant stereotyping that keep them locked in boxes of the surrounding society's imagination which don't reflect each person's actual lived experience. Many people have what they consider non-negative "positive" stereotypes as well. In all circumstances, although the intent may be to complement rather than tear down ("All Asians are violin players..." and "All African Americans are great basketball players"), they are still generalizations that have negative effects. Many stereotypes are based on historical narratives deeply embedded in U.S. society.

Those narratives include stories about North America's rationalized "conquest" of Indians. It made Indians seem primitive (an inferior race), warlike (inherently violent), stupid (because they had no recognizable literate culture), and slothful.

THE "REAL INDIAN STEREOTYPE"

The concept of the real Indian is one of the most ubiquitous of all stereotypes created by the U.S. government's policy that suggested that only "pure-blooded" Indians were "real Indians," and others who married out of the Indian community became "half-bloods" or "quarter-bloods" and thus evolved away from being an Indian. A "real" Indian conforms to various ideals or concepts inherent in common stereotypes.

Directions: Please answer the questions.

Think about what you consider a "real" Indian to be, and make a list of his or her characteristics or qualities.

_____

_____

Do you know any American Indian people? If you do, how well do they match your list? Do they conform to your mental image of what a "real" Indian looks like, dresses like, talks like, and acts like?

_____

_____

If you don't know any Native people, how realistic do you think your list is? Is your list based on actual knowledge of today's Native realities, or is it based more on stereotypical images you've been influenced by?

_____

_____

Have you ever asked these questions or heard these statements?

"How much Indian blood do you have?"

What's wrong with this question?

_____

_____

"What part Indian are you?"

What's wrong with this comment?

_____

_____

_____

"You don't look Indian!"

What's wrong with this question?

_____

_____

_____

One assumes that a person is supposed to have some specific set of physical characteristics—most usually a stereotypical Lakota person with long braids. Substitute the word "Russian," "English," or "Italian" for the word "Indian" to see how truly silly this comment is.

"What is your animal totem?"

What's wrong with this question?

_____

_____

_____

"What is the meaning of a butterfly on my shoulder?"

What's wrong with this question?

_____

_____

_____

EXERCISE
ASIAN STEREOTYPE AWARENESS

Ethnic stereotypes can interfere with the process of positive identity formation and can foster doubts that become internalized as depression, dissociation, and self-harm.

Directions: As you read through these common Asian stereotypes explore your own reactions.

• Asians are brainiacs, over-achievers and are naturally gifted at math and medicine.

• Asian children are born to be scholars.

• Asian students are taking over college admissions.

• Asian men never marry non-Asian women.

• Asian women are exotic, passive and sexy – until a certain age, when they all of a sudden lose their magic and transform into hunch-backed, gap-toothed crones.

• Asian men are sexually emasculated because they have almost no body hair and tiny genitals.

• Asian women covet large wide eyes with two creases in their eyelids, and feel ashamed about their small eyes.

• Asians all look the same.

• Asians eat weird foods such as shark's fin, dog, cat, all kinds of insects, seaweed, raw meat, chicken feet, duck embryo, black eggs packaged as 'centuries old.'

• Asians are Kung Fu masters and live by Confucian truisms.

• Eastern cultures are ancient while Western cultures are modern – except in the Japanese metropolis, where hi-tech robotics reign.

MODEL MINORITY EXERCISE

Consider the list of Asian stereotypes: what do you think when you hear the word "model minority" or "positive stereotypes"?

_____

_____

_____

_____

_____

_____

_____

What are some of the "positive stereotypes" that you believe?

_____

_____

_____

_____

_____

_____

_____

_____

BEING UNDERSTOOD AS A MULTIRACIAL OR MULTICULTURAL PERSON

Directions: People who are multiracial or have been raised in multicultural home have a unique story to share. To better understand their background, ask your client the following questions, or have them complete the worksheet.

How do you define your cultural/ethnic background?

_____

_____

_____

_____

How were you raised culturally and in what ways did the cultures influence who you are?

_____

_____

_____

_____

Did you feel misunderstood because of your bicultural background?

_____

_____

_____

_____

What are the positive aspects of this dual identity?

_____

_____

_____

_____

How central is it to how you identify?

_____

_____

_____

_____

Have you faced problems or challenges because of your bicultural identity?

_____

_____

_____

_____

Did you struggle with connecting with the different cultural communities of your parents?

_____

_____

_____

_____

Do you think that if you were only one ethnicity that things would be simpler or easier? Why or why not?

_____

_____

_____

_____

RESOURCES

Access many of these resources online at www.healthalt.org

Books and Publications

Bellegarde-Smith, P. (Ed.)(2005.) *Fragments of Bone: Neo-African Religions in a New World.* Santa Barbara, CA: Center for Black Studies Research.

Bellegarde-Smith, P. (Ed.).(2007). *Haitian Vodou: Spirit, Myth & Reality.* Bloomington, IN: Indiana University Press.

CodeSwitch: Frontiers of Race, Culture, and Ethnicity. A team of journalists fascinated by the overlapping themes of race, ethnicity and culture, how they play out in our lives and communities, and how all of this is shifting. http://www.npr.org/blogs/codeswitch/2014/08/09/338974310/are-you-like-african-american-or-african-american

Carney, Judith. (2011) *In the Shadow of Slavery: Africa's Botanical Legacy in the Atlantic World.* Oakland, CA: University of California Press.

Gaines, Stanley O., Jr. (1997). *Culture, Ethnicity, and Personal Relationship Processes,* London: Routledge.

Galland, C. (1991) *Longing for Darkness: Tara and the Black Madonna.* West Minster, London: Penguin Books

Gruenewald, M. M. (2005). *Looking Like the Enemy: My Story of Imprisonment in Japanese American Internment Camps.* Troutdale, Oregon: New Sage Press

Hucks, T. E. (2012). *Yoruba Traditions and African American Religious Nationalism.* University of New Mexico Press. Albuquerque, New Mexico

Explores the Yoruba Tradition in the United States

Hurston, Zora, N. (1999). *Mules and Men.* New York, NY: Harper Perennial.

Contains folklore stories and tales of medicine and magic.

Irish America Magazine

Each bi-monthly issue of Irish America celebrates the resurgence of Irish heritage among Irish Americans

http://irishamerica.com/who-we-are/about-the-magazine/

Shirley Jones,(1999). Simply Living: The Spirit of the Indigenous People. Novato, CA: New World Library. We all carry within us the ancient, tribal identity of indigenous people—people native to their lands. As technology continues to dominate and complicate modern life, many are striving to reclaim that tribal connection by living more simply.

Shook, Victoria E. (1986). *Ho 'oponopono: Contemporary Uses of a Hawaiian Problem Solving Process,* Honolulu, Hawaii: University of Hawaii Press.

Sue, S. (2009).Ethnic minority psychology: Struggles and triumphs." *Cultural Diversity & Ethnic Minority Psychology, 15,* 4, 409-415

Trotter, R. T., & J. A. Chavira. (1997). *Curanderismo, Mexican American Folk Healing.* A classic book about *curanderismo*; covers its history, modern-day relevance in Mexico and the United States. Also includes photographs. Athens, Georgia: University of Georgia Press.

The Historical Loss Scale

Whitbeck LB, Adams GW, Hoyt DR, Chen X. (2004) *Conceptualizing and Measuring Historical Trauma among American Indian People.* American Journal of Community Psychology June;33(3-4):119-30.

This scale measures how often thoughts pertaining to historical loss occur. It has been used among North American Indigenous populations.

Movies/Videos
American Fusion
A romantic comedy about stereotypes and family relationships.

Bound: African versus African Americans:
A documentary that addresses the little-known tension that exists between Africans and African Americans.

The Bridge
Award-winning show depicting violent story line and realistic relationships among police on both sides of the Mexican American Border.

Finding Your Roots: Learn about the Rochon Family
http://www.pbslearningmedia.org/resource/fyr14.socst.us.rochon/the-rochons-an-african-american-dynasty/

PBS has a variety of resources on Mexico and Mexican American History and Stories

Mexican American History
http://www.pbs.org/opb/historydetectives/feature/mexican-americans/

The Mexican American War
http://www.pbs.org/kera/usmexicanwar/timeline_flash.html

Real Women Have Curves: Award-winning coming of age film about a Mexican American teenager living in East L.A.)

Sin Nombre, a teen immigration story

The Gangs of New York tells the story of the turn of the century migration of Irish to New York

The Irish in America: Long Journey Home: The Great Hunger (PBS)
https://www.youtube.com/watch?v=xONqZXzQ1yY

The Three Burials of Melquiades Estrada
The Other Side of Immigration
A documentary that focuses on interviews with Mexicans living both in Mexico and the United States in order to understand the underlying reasons people are motivated to emigrate.

Music
Hearth Sounds: Ancient Songs from Ireland and the World
http://www.soundstrue.com/store/hearth-sounds.html

Mana
Maná is a Mexican rock band. To access information and music
http://www.mana.com.mx/en

Organizations
Annual ArabFest (festivals) are held throughout major US cities to celebrate and share Arab cultures through food, dance arts and music

The Congress of Santa Barbara and the Scholarly Association for the Study of Haitian Vodou, holds an annual academic congress to explore all facets of Vodou.
http://www.research.ucsb.edu/cbs/projects/haiti/kosanba/

Incantations by Mayan Women
A publishing collective operated by contemporary Mayan artists in Chiapas, Mexico. Creates the first books to be written, illustrated, printed, bound (in paper of their own making) by Mayan people in over 400 years.
http://www.tallerlenateros.com/ingles/index_ing.php

Irish American Cultural Institute
Founded in 1962, the Irish American Cultural Institute (IACI) is the leading Irish American cultural organization. http://www.iaci-usa.org/home.html

Poetry
"Asian spoken word" http://www.theasiaproject.com/poetry/home.php

Web Resources
Culture Heritage Tours
Many companies offer heritage and family tree tours that include visits to geneology museums and visits to local areas to identify your roots.
http://www.cultureheritagetours.ie/

Hyphen: Asian American Arts Culture and Politics (Weblog)
http://www.hyphenmagazine.com/blog/archive/2012/10/science-racism-radiolabs-treatment-hmong-experience

In Motion: The African-American Migration Experience. Presents a new interpretation of African-American history, one that focuses on the self-motivated activities of peoples of African descent to remake themselves and their worlds. http://www.inmotionaame.org/home.cfm

Interviews and audio programming related to many aspects of the Mexican-American experience, including *curanderismo* and issues surrounding migration
http://www.laits.utexas.edu/onda_latina/index

Pew Hispanic
Current issues in Mexican immigration as well as important statistical data
http://www.pewhispanic.org/

Yoruba Practice
Listen to a story of current Yoruba practice.
http://www.npr.org/2013/08/25/215298340/ancient-african-religion-finds-roots-in-america

Vodou - With Bellegarde-Smith, Haitian Philosopher, Vodou priest, and a professor at the University of Wisconsin in Milwaukee.
http://www.onbeing.org/program/living-vodou/transcript/989

Terms
"African American" and "Black" http://www.nytimes.com/2004/08/29/us/african-american-becomes-a-term-for-debate.html
"Hispanic" and "Latino/a": http://www.pewhispanic.org/2009/05/28/whos-hispanic/

Chapter 5
Religion & Spirituality

Chapter 5
Religion & Spirituality

"The lamps are different, but the light is the same."

— Jalalu'l-Din Rumi, Sufi poet and mystic

While ideas and opinions about gender and sexuality summon vigorous debate, nothing evokes more discussion than the role of spirituality and religion in the counseling of mental health and physical health. Eighty percent of the U.S. population practices some sort of religion or spirituality and yet the topic causes considerable controversy. Moreover, while the majority of clients want to be able to discuss religion and spirituality with their clinicians, often they are afraid to raise the issue or clinicians are uncomfortable with the discussion.

Because religious practices derive from belief systems, religion often plays an important role in life decisions that will enter into the clinical setting. It may influence decisions about pregnancy, child rearing, abortion, end of life care, sexuality and gender identity. Thus our own comfort as clinicians with all aspects of religion and spirituality will enhance our capacity to support client well-being.

Spirituality is frequently confused with religion. While a religion may call upon spirituality as an expression of transcendence, spirituality involves a dimension that inspires and seeks balance in the universe. When a person experiences emotional, mental or physical stress he or she may seek transcendent meaning in music, art, nature and, yes, in philosophical understanding. How do we integrate spirituality into treatment? Is it necessary? Religion is another matter. What if we are atheist? How do we address religion with a client? What if our beliefs are radically different from our client's? How do we distinguish the beneficial effects of religion from the destructive? How do we treat a survivor of religious or cult abuse? Spirituality, as distinct from organized religion, frequently becomes a topic of concern in the counseling session.

 There are many definitions of religion and spirituality. The most important definition is the client's, so ask your client:

What does religion and spirituality mean to you?

RELIGION VS. SPIRITUALITY

Religion
In Latin the word *religio* means obligation or bond.

Spirituality
The root of spirituality derives from the word *respirar,* meaning to breathe. Many spiritual practices are rooted in breathing—the link between the inner and outer worlds.

One yogic saying suggests: "To control the breath is to control the mind," hence the integration of breath control and CBT to enhance mental well-being. Whereas religion often refers to an organized set of practices and ideological beliefs or doctrines, spirituality often refers more to the meaning and purpose of the individual self in relation to the larger whole. Spirituality can be useful as it relates to recovery of health and well-being. For example, posttraumatic growth is linked to spirituality. Thus it may be useful to cultivate spiritual practices during stressful or traumatic events.

Religiosity

Refers to the state of being religious, however more often it is used to denote an exaggerated embodiment of certain aspects of religious activity that can lead to obsessive practice, and denial or judgement of others. Some studies suggest that religion is an effective coping mechanism for stress and depression while others demonstrate higher rates of depression and anxiety among people who practice religion. It may also be that illness engenders a search for meaning.

Transpersonal

Refers to "beyond the personal." It is a field of psychology, also called spiritual psychology. Transpersonal psychology explores psychological experience in the context of a wide range of spiritual phenomena including mystical and religious experiences, altered states of consciousness, anomalous experiences, also paranormal or psychic phenomena such as telepathy, "peak flow" experiences, and contemplative practice.

CONTROVERSIAL ASPECTS OF RELIGION AND SPIRITUAL BELIEFS

There are a number of ideas held by people who consider themselves religious that lead to oppressive behaviors against others. These can have detrimental effects on mental and physical well-being, LGBTQ, and women's rights.

Almost all types of religions can be used to support oppressive beliefs and behaviors toward others but among the most common are some sects of Christianity, Mormon/LDS, Orthodox Judaism, and Islam. While Hindusim does not consider homosexuality a sin some sects of Buddhism and Skihism do. Among these beliefs are:

- LGBTQ people are immoral or sinful or that their sexual relationships are sinful.
- Conversion therapy (also called reparative therapy) can help people who identify at LGBTQ to become heterosexual. No major mental health and medical professional association supports this therapy and significant research suggests it has harmful results if attempted.

This points to the need to understand and explore the various sects or spectrums of all the religions, some of which are more conservative or fundamentalist, and others more progressive. All religious institutions now have organizational resources that address the needs of their LGBTQ members. For example, while homosexuality is considered against the precepts of Mormonism, a Mormon Gay and Lesbian organization called Affirmation (http://affirmation.org/) comprises of Mormon or formerly Mormon LGBTQ members.

In 2009, President Jimmy Carter, a Nobel Peace laureate and deeply religious man by his own account severed his lifelong ties with the Southern Baptist Church over their official policies that included that women should be subservient to men. In his letter he stated:

"This discrimination, unjustifiably attributed to a Higher Authority, has provided a reason or excuse for the deprivation of women's equal rights across the world for centuries. At its

most repugnant, the belief that women must be subjugated to the wishes of men excuses slavery, violence, forced prostitution, genital mutilation and national laws that omit rape as a crime. But it also costs many millions of girls and women control over their own bodies and lives, and continues to deny them fair access to education, health, employment and influence within their own communities. The same discriminatory thinking lies behind the continuing gender gap in pay and why there are still so few women in office in the West. The root of this prejudice lies deep in our histories, but its impact is felt every day. It is not women and girls alone who suffer. It damages all of us."

To read the full letter:
http://www.theage.com.au/federal-politics/losing-my-religion-for-equality-20090714-dk0v.html

Clergy Sexual Abuse

While the Catholic Church has been publically scrutinized for the systemic sexual and physical abuse of children and adults by priests, every organized religion or spiritual group has been found to have predators and pedophiles who abuse their adherents. In particular, religion is often used to justify the abuse and this leads to significant trauma and often a loss of faith and hope in the greater good. People in recovery from sexual abuse by trusted clergy often leave the religion or group, and coming to terms with a new belief system often becomes part of the treatment process with mental health clinicians. It is important to inquire sensitively about such experiences in religious and spiritual institutions as often victims experience confusion and shame, and may not fully understand what has happened to them and thus may not reveal their experiences to the clinician at first.

Religion, Cult and Mind Control

It is important to ascertain the specific ways religion is being used to cope. In my own practice, I differentiate between people who define their religious or spiritual practice and those who are defined by it. Religious or spiritual organizations may also be a cult and conduct mind control. Mind control is referred to as the "manipulation of attachment needs" and is used to control people's behavior, often by enacting trance and dissociative states. There are many survivors of mind control and cult control, whether by large organized religions or by so-called fringe religions. Control is often exerted for the purpose of obtaining resources from the adherent, whether it be financial, sexual or other forms of ego gratification.

It is important to explore history and present practices with clients since, as with sexual abuse, people are often in denial, or have repressed memories that continue, nonetheless to drive self-destructive behaviors or chronic mood disorders.

RELIGION/SPIRITUALITY

Directions: Supporting our clients' interest in religion and spirituality requires that we explore our own beliefs and attitudes. Complete this exercise alone or with colleagues.

Were you raised in a religious or spiritual tradition?

_____

_____

_____

_____

_____

Do you still practice it? If not, why? If so, have you made any changes?

_____

_____

_____

_____

_____

_____

In what ways does your practice have meaning for you?

_____

_____

_____

_____

_____

When you have a client from a religious background that is different from yours, how do you respond?

_____

_____

_____

_____

_____

How do you describe your beliefs if a client asks?

_____

_____

_____

_____

_____

If you identify as atheist or agnostic how do you respond to a client who asks you about your religious beliefs?

_____

_____

_____

_____

_____

_____

_____

_____

RELIGION AND SPIRITUAL BELIEFS

Directions: Complete this exercise alone or with colleagues.

Think about your own religious beliefs or spiritual beliefs or atheist beliefs. Have you experienced stress as a result of those beliefs?

_____

_____

_____

_____

Think of a religion you know little about but have strong feelings or ideas about. What are your attitudes about it? How did you develop these feelings and ideas?

_____

_____

_____

_____

Think about your beliefs about a religion that is not your own. List three negative beliefs and three positive beliefs.

_____

_____

_____

_____

_____

_____

RELIGION, SPIRITUALITY AND MICROAGGRESSIONS

In Chapter 2 we explored the concept of microaggression as it relates to culture and ethnicity. Below explore the concepts of microaggressions as they relate to religious and spiritual beliefs.

Endorsing Religious Stereotypes —Statements or behaviors that communicate false, presumptuous, or incorrect perceptions of certain religious groups (e.g., stereotyping that a Muslim person is a terrorist or that a Jewish person is cheap).

Exoticization—Instances where people view other religions as trendy or foreign (e.g., an individual who dresses in a certain religion's garb or garments for fashion or pleasure).

Pathologization of Different Religious Groups —Statements and behaviors in which individuals equate certain religious practices or traditions as being abnormal, sinful, or deviant (e.g., telling someone that they are in the "wrong" religion).

Assumption of One's Own Religious Identity as the Norm —Comments or behaviors that convey people's presumption that their religion is the standard (e.g., saying, "Merry Christmas" or "God bless you" after someone sneezes conveys one's perception that everyone is Christian or believes in God).

Assumption of Religious Homogeneity —Statements in which individuals assume that every believer of a religion practices the same customs or has the same beliefs as the entire group (e.g., assuming that all Muslim people wear head coverings).

Denial of Religious Prejudice —Incidents in which individuals claim that they are not religiously biased, even if their words or behaviors may indicate otherwise.

SPIRITUALITY AND TRAUMA RECOVERY

Spirituality can play an integral role in post-trauma therapy and addiction recovery. Spirituality and religion contribute to personal and community beliefs about the trauma and to the potential for making meaning. The role of spirituality and religion in a client's life should be assessed early so that we can find ways to integrate it at each stage of recovery. Engaging spirituality in posttraumatic therapy requires assessing and understanding pre-trauma beliefs and practices as well as the effects of the trauma on spirituality. Spirituality and religion will have different definitions for people, and understanding what people mean by these terms is an important starting point. This information can be obtained during the initial assessment or during the early stages of treatment in exploring strategies for self-care and social supports.

Transpersonal (beyond the personal) psychotherapy helps address the needs of the trauma victim regardless of organized religious practice by addressing the loss of hope and meaning

When traumatic experience is human-mediated, it often leads to the exploration of questions of good and evil, karma, fate and predestination and other religious and philosophical ideas. I always ask my clients, at an appropriate point in our work together:

> • *Do you have a spiritual or religious practice? If so, can you tell me about it?*
> • *Do you see yourself as a spiritual or religious person?*
> • *Is there a role of spirituality in your recovery process?*
> • *What has helped you to survive the traumas you experienced?*

From there we can explore the client's practices and, the role of religion and spirituality in coping with stress and making meaning out of their experiences. The client may also discuss anomalous experiences such as altered states, or religious visions they have experienced.

Together we can create a spiritual genogram, which is useful to explore intergenerational relationships regarding religion and spirituality and can be added to a family genogram.

If the trauma is associated with, or results from, a religious experience or affiliation—such as clergy abuse or abuse by a guru—that trauma provides a new dimension to explore.

When victims have been abused by a spiritual leader, guru, or clergy member who has introduced them to prayer or meditation, they may experience ambivalence about religion and spirituality, especially if religious doctrine or spiritual methods were used as a form of mind control. This type of trauma is also called betrayal trauma.

Debbie

Debbie entered therapy because she was depressed and had debilitating headaches for which no organic cause had been established. During the second interview, I asked her if she had ever prayed or meditated, and she responded that she was no longer able to pray. She began to tell her story of abuse by her pastor, who told her that they had to pray together in order for her to heal from cancer. He insisted that she take her clothes off and let him fondle her while she prayed, for it would "strengthen her message to God."

Now, 10 years later, she entered therapy, confused about this experience and not wanting to "talk to God." The first step was to affirm that what had happened was inappropriate and abusive and could very possibly be causing her depression and headaches. We explored relaxation techniques that did not remind her of prayer or meditation, and I referred her for cranial sacral therapy, which provided effective, gentle hands-on treatment for her headaches.

During our work together, which spanned five years, Debbie processed the memories of her experience and the ways in which the pastor had "stolen her spirit" from her. This included her loss of innocence and her trust in the church and in God, her resulting difficulties with sexuality, and a debilitating depression that had prevented her from achieving the career goals she held in her heart. She grieved over many losses and, toward the end of our work, decided to experiment with some new forms of prayer and meditation. She then started a secular group of people interested in spirituality.

THERAPIST WORKSHEET
RELIGION ATTITUDES AND BELIEFS

Directions: For this exercise, pick a religion or sect that you have strong feelings about or perhaps know little about but have heard ideas about (e.g., Jewish, Sikh, Catholic, Protestant, Muslim.)

_____

Allow your stream of consciousness to flow, and identify the first words that rise to your awareness. The first images that come to mind when I think about this religion:

_____

_____

The first images I see in my mind's eye when I think of people who are in this religion:

_____

_____

The obstacles I might experience working with someone with these religious or spiritual beliefs:

_____

_____

My next steps to educate myself about this belief system are:

_____

_____

Do I need to refer someone with these beliefs to another practitioner? If so how would I make this referral? What would I say?

_____

_____

CHRISTIANITY

In the U.S., 70% of the population identifies as Christian. 25% percent of the Christian population identifies as evangelical and 6.5% are historically Black Protestants. While Christianity is associated with the rise of the Roman Catholic Church one must take into consideration breakaway; denominations that have become separate entities.

Mental Health and Christians

While faith can be an important aspect of mental wellness, it can also contribute to a level of psychological distress. For example, some research shows that among conservative Protestants not attending church or not reading religious scripture as much as their peers contributes to higher levels of psychological distress. Other stressors can be a sense of embarrassment in front of other believers, or the fear that seeking treatment from non-Christians will erode one's faith.

For clinicians whose worldview is different from that of their Christian clients, building an effective client/therapist relationship can be more challenging. Christians want to know that the counselor will take their faith seriously. Christian individuals often want counseling from people who understand their faith and can counsel from that perspective. This is called Christian counseling or faith-based counseling. Christian counseling begins with the assumption that there is a distinction between psychotherapy that is grounded in Christian principles and that which is not grounded in Christian principles. Research suggests that women and African Americans in particular value faith-based counseling and will seek counselors who integrate their faith into counseling.

> **Did you know?**
>
> The term WASP stands for White (or Wealthy) Anglo Saxon Protestant. While it may have begun as a purely descriptive term for people who were white people from England, over the years it has become a term of disparagement. Stereotypes of WASP include wealthy, arrogant, power hungry, tightlipped, stoic, and privately-educated.

Christian counseling approaches run along a spectrum that describes varying degrees of conservative and more liberal views. On the more conservative end, Pentecostals and Fundamentalists view psychiatric illness as the manifestation of a spiritual problem which only a pastor or Christian counselor is capable of addressing. Adherence to prayer, Bible reading, and other instruction are the primary treatment modalities. More liberal views include viewing spiritual health and mental health as interdependent without one being prioritized.

Clinicians should use language that relates to the client's religious orientation. Questions about faith, such as asking about the client's salvation experience may help connect to a particular frame of reference. Clinicians should be careful not to criticize the client's religious perspective, even when they've expressed doubt, and feelings should be validated. Consultation or collaboration with clergy can be effective in helping with spiritual issues or with mental health concerns where spiritual practice can be a source for coping and change behaviors.

Advocacy, Social Justice and Religion

As mental health clinicians, our ethical duty is to advocate for our clients and understand the role of social injustice as a contributing factor in poor mental health. Advocacy has a long history as part of religious practice. Clergy from many religions, often working without the sanction of their churches, have a long tradition of social justice activities such as the protests of the Berrigans and William Sloane Coffin against the Vietnam war and the tradition of liberation theology which evolved in Latin America in the 1950s in response to poverty and social oppression.

Catholic priests, nuns and lay members, often working against the official sanction of the Church have a tradition of social justice activities called Liberation Theology. Liberation Theology evolved during the 1950's in Latin America in response to poverty and social oppression. Liberation theology has been adapted by many activist theologians who draw from the original teachings of Christ in support of the poor. Feminist Liberation theologians such as Rosemary Ruether, Elizabeth Schussler-Fiorenza and Letty Russell focus on gender, and the oppression of women in society and the equal status of religious Christian women. Ignacio Martín-Baró was a Jesuit priest and psychologist who contributed to the concepts of liberation theology. He was murdered in El Salvador in 1989.

ISLAM

Who are Muslims?

Muslim is a word used to describe the followers of Islam. Almost one-fourth of the world's population is Muslim. In the U.S., 32% of the Muslim population is South Asian, with 26% Arab-speaking, and 20% African American. Contrary to popular belief, the majority of people from the Middle East living in the U.S. are Christian, not Muslim.

As with most religions, beliefs and practices among Muslim people vary in degree of conservative or "traditional" to liberal or "progressive" interpretations of religious practice and beliefs. The holy book is called the Koran (also commonly spelled Quran in English). There are two main branches of Islam: Sunni and Shi'ite. The largest number of the 1.3 billion practitioners of Islam are Sunni.

Though all Muslims agree about the divine mission of Mohammed, the rift between the two primary Islamic sects is rooted in a dispute about who rightfully carried on Mohammed's word and work. Shi'ites believe that only the prophet's blood relatives have such a right to religious governance whereas the Sunni's believe that a religious leader can be elected to represent the teachings.

Shi'ites: The more devout, and some say, conservative Muslims, the Shi'ites, read the Koran daily and enter into prayer five times a day facing towards Mecca. Women wear veils, fast ritually, and must make a pilgrimage called Hajj to the holy land (Mecca) at least once in their lifetime.

Sunnis: The majority of Muslims have adapted their practice to suit a modern humanist culture. Many frequently read the Koran and if women wear veils, it is by choice. They may visit Mecca (Hajj) once in their lifetime. Like Shi'ites, Sunnis observe Ramadan: a strict month of fasting from dawn to dusk.

Sufi: As in Judaism and Christianity there is also a mystical aspect to Islam. The practice of mysticism is an experiential approach that reinforces the personal experience of the deity. In Islam spiritual mystics are called Sufis. They are devout Muslims who are on a sacred mission to embody Allah through meditation, prayer, fasting, dance and flagellation. The "Whirling Dervishes are Sufi's who are known for their whirling dances that represent an ecstatic spiritual practice. UNESCO recognized their ceremony called *Mevlevi Sema* as a cultural heritage to humanity.

Mental Health and Muslims

Among the major factors contributing to stress and mental illness among Muslim individuals and families include recent immigration from other countries and the experience of war and other traumatic events. These war traumas may include betrayal and mistrust and thus group counseling may not be warranted or as effective as individual counseling (Nasser-MacMillian& Hakim-Larson 2003). Other stressors leading to mental issues include discrimination, bigotry and hate crimes resulting from the after effects of 9/11 and the "War on Terror" in which (some of) the media has targeted Muslims. The stress of gender relationships, domestic violence, adapting to U.S. culture and integrating that with Muslim practices and values can also cause significant stress for Muslim clients.

ISLAM & MUSLIM PERCEPTIONS

Directions: Please answer the following questions.

What do you think about when you hear the word Muslim?

_____

_____

_____

_____

Do you have any Muslim friends?

_____

_____

_____

_____

Have you ever spoken to a Muslim about their religion and beliefs?

_____

_____

_____

_____

In the United States there has been a significant backlash against people who identify as Muslim, associating Islam with anti-American and terrorist activities. What do you know about this backlash? What have you read or observed? How has the media influenced your understanding of Islam?

_____

_____

_____

_____

_____

Islamic Cultural Awareness

It is important to for us to identify and process assumptions based on inaccurate information or internalized stereotypes. As is true in many religious contexts, Islam is both a religion and a culture. Evidence suggests that members of the Muslim faith tend to seek help from faith-based sources for psychiatric and emotional problems. Often the help provided by clergy can be enough, but some problems require mental health professionals, some of whom may be outside the Muslim community. While there are Muslim mental health providers(many of whom are bi and tri lingual) in communities that have a sizable population of Muslims, there are some areas of the country with no Muslim health professionals.

Islamic beliefs about illness are closely linked to beliefs about God (Allah) and *kader* (also spelled Qadar) which refers to one's fate or destiny. Allah is regarded as both the cause and the healer of illness; it may be a test or a punishment. Mental illness in particular may be perceived as a test or punishment, is highly stigmatized, and often characterized by shame. Self-stigma is the biggest barrier to accessing mental health services. Additionally, Muslim women express higher need for mental health services compared to men, who have more negative attitudes toward seeking help. Like many belief systems that stigmatize mental health more than physical health, emotional distress is often *somatized*. Thus the clinician should be sensitive to the meaning of illness and the "narrative" of the symptoms.

Islamic culture is based on certain tenets derived from the teachings of the Koran and the Prophet Muhammad. Depending on the denomination, other principles may be primary as well, such as the *Sunnah* (prescribed way of life) and the *Hadith* (the prophetic tradition). While specific beliefs may vary along denominational lines, certain qualities can be said to be common among all (or most) Muslims. For example, one of the most common elements is the commitment to modesty called Hayaa' and simplicity.

Modesty is the basis for the headscarf worn by women, which has different names and styles depending on country and denomination. In the West the most common headscarf, cover or veil is the *hijab (pronounced hee-jub)*. It is often negatively perceived as emblematic of gender inequality. Although in some countries this may be true, in the West women often adopt it as a sign of their Muslim identity, both spiritually and culturally. Thus, the meaning of the hijab should be explored with the individual woman.

ISLAMIC CULTURAL AWARENESS

Directions: Please answer the following questions.

When you see a woman wearing a hijab, what are your initial thoughts and impressions?

_____

_____

_____

_____

What influences are these feelings or ideas based on?

_____

_____

_____

_____

Do you find yourself thinking about images from news broadcasts or movies about the 9/11 World Trade Center bombings or other politically charged media?

_____

_____

_____

_____

Are you aware that turbans (worn by males) are not a Muslim practice, but from the Sikh tradition? What do you know about the difference between Sikhs and Muslims? (Sikhs have also been exposed to hate crimes, mistaken for Muslim men.)

_____

_____

_____

_____

Consider the religion that you are most familiar with. What has been your experience along the conservative/liberal spectrum?

_____

_____

_____

_____

_____

_____

_____

_____

_____

_____

_____

_____

Have you ever been to any Muslim cultural events, or traveled to a Muslim country? If so describe your experiences. If not, where would you propose to visit and why?

_____

_____

_____

_____

_____

_____

_____

_____

_____

MUSLIM PRIDE EXERCISE

Directions: Ask your client to describe their experience of being Muslim in a non-Muslim country. Ask for details:

- *Were you born into a Muslim family or did you convert?*

- *If you converted, how did your family respond to the conversion?*

- *Was there support, ridicule, or indifference?*

- *Have you experienced bigotry? If so, in what ways?*

- *Have you taken the hajj (pilgrimage to Mecca); would you like to?*

Invite your client to make a collage with photos, documents, mementos or other symbols of their faith. This is a symbolic representation of their personal spiritual journey.

This exercise can be carried out with anyone. Keep in mind the Muslim value of modesty, and first make sure that such a project won't be perceived as an affront to their belief system.

WORKSHEET
ISLAM, MARRIAGE AND MOTHERHOOD

Like those from many religions, women with Muslim heritage have intense pressure to marry a partner who practices the Islamic faith. As in most all cultures and religions, the social contract called marriage can be a point of tension that can result in the oppression of women and the denial of their rights for the sake of preserving tradition. This can be exacerbated when people emigrate from one country to another and when generational differences exist.

People often seek counseling during these "pressure points" yet may also feel hesitant to identify the root problem.

How we respond to our clients' challenges around marriage and gender/cultural/religious roles may be influenced by our own earlier experiences.

Directions: The clinician or the client may answer the questions below.

Did you or do you feel pressure to keep the peace in your family and follow tradition?

_____

_____

_____

_____

_____

Are you a child who is pressured to pass on family lineage?

_____

_____

_____

_____

_____

_____

_____

Do you feel like there is an intergenerational conflict between the individualist mentality of the present and the community/family emphasis of your religion?

_____

_____

_____

_____

Do you think that religion means different things to your parents and to you?

_____

_____

_____

_____

_____

To your children?

_____

_____

_____

_____

Do you feel like you can peacefully engage your parents on the subject of religious difference? In what ways can you? What might be the obstacles?

_____

_____

_____

_____

_____

WORKSHEET
FILIAL PIETY

Filial piety means to be good to one's parents and uphold respect to one's ancestors. To not be rebellious, but show love and respect, to support one's parents (either materially or through wise advice to help them do what is right), to uphold peace between siblings, to be courteous and socially graceful.

Yet American popular culture revels in audacious tales of teenage rebellion. Coming-of-age stories are launched by the rejection of parental values. Indeed in psychology we consider this a natural, developmental stage of the individuation process. Yet this process can be seen to undermine some traditional religious or cultural values where filial piety is seen as less of a "chore" than a deeply held responsibility to obey and keep communication alive between the generations.

Directions: To discuss something with parents with filial piety means to be honest and genuine. It means to honor family integrity overall and to avoid all-or-nothing situations. Think about this concept and answer the following questions:

What are your values regarding filial piety?

_____

_____

Do they align or conflict with those of your parents? Your siblings?

_____

_____

Can you bring alignment to these values and enhance connection within your family? If so, what do you need to do so?

_____

_____

THERAPIST WORKSHEET

ISLAMOPHOBIA

Islamophobia refers to prejudice against, or fear of Muslims and the religion of Islam. It is also understood as a type of social anxiety and social stigma about Islam and Muslims. Islamophobia has been on the rise since 2001 and can contribute to stress and poor mental health among Muslim individuals and families.

Directions: Please answer the following questions:

List a few ways in which you have observed Islamophobia; In yourself, in others? In the media?

_____

_____

_____

What are some of the factors that contribute to Islamophobia?

_____

_____

_____

How would you address Islamophobia expressed by a client?

_____

_____

_____

What might you as a clinician do to advocate community actions or ideas to your clients to reduce Islamophobia?

_____

_____

_____

ART THERAPY: MAKING A RAMADAN PAPER MOBILE

Directions: This exercise can be done by anyone, but is especially useful when working with children. It is also a good activity to share during family therapy. Children and adults alike often feel more at ease talking about feelings when constructing an art project. During this project one can discuss concerns of any type but may also focus on feelings and experiences related to spirituality, religion, and relationships.

Ramadan is the most sacred month in Islamic tradition, It is a celebration that includes prayer and fasting. Ramadan begins in the ninth lunar month of the Islamic calendar. Check for a list of dates of Ramadan's upcoming years on the Internet.

In this exercise the client will make a simple paper mobile of a crescent moon and stars. The base of the mobile is a large crescent moon from which will dangle stars.

Materials

- Scissors
- Plain paper
- Pencil
- Colorful paper (card stock is best); big craft stores will carry a large selection of beautiful papers. Use your imagination.
- Pipe cleaners
- Colorful yarn or other string
- Glue
- Glitter
- Hole punch

This mobile can be made either at home or in your office. If your client makes it at home, have her bring in and explain the elements and what they mean to her. Have her talk about Ramadan memories of her childhood and other family activities associated with the holiday.

Directions

1. On the plain paper draw 2 shapes, one that is a large crescent moon, and another of a star (you can have different sizes if you like). These are the templates. The stars will be smaller and will hang from the moon. They can also hang from each other in any configuration desired.

2. Use the template to draw the designs on your colored paper and cut out.

3. Once the designs are cut out they can be decorated with the glitter.

4. Spread the glue on the paper moon and stars and sprinkle with glitter.

5. After the glue is dry, punch one small hole at the top and one or more holes base of the moon.

6. Punch holes at the top of each star.

7. Join the stars to the moon and to each other with the pipe cleaners or yarn.

8. Cut a piece of yarn for the top of the moon; this will be what the mobile will hang from.

An alternative to making a decorative mobile, is to ask you client to talk about Ramadan memories from childhood and other family activities associated with the holiday. The goal is to promote a sense of pride about the client's cultural and religious heritage and also support a deeper dialogue about meaning in one's life.

HINDUISM

Hinduism in its broadest form is practiced by 80% of India's population with an additional 30 million living outside India, making Hinduism the third largest religion in the world following Christianity and Islam. Hinduism is not a unified or homogenous religion. It does not have a founder but relies on sacred texts that are interpreted in many different ways resulting in many different Hindu traditions. Hindu followers refer to the religion as "dharma" or "eternal religion." The first writing has been dated to 3,200 years before the present. Buddhism and Jainism are thought to have emerged from Hinduism about 2,500 years ago.

Approximately 0.7% of the U.S. population is Hindu, with the majority of Hindus immigrants from India and a small number of converts. The Hindu population is among the most highly educated in the U.S.

Hinduism includes the beliefs of karma and reincarnation, which have become integrated into mainstream language and ideas among popular culture and "New Age" systems. Karma suggests that every thought, word and action affects current and future lives.

Hindu beliefs and practices vary widely, and practices tend to reflect the culture where it is practiced. This is also reflected in relationships between men and women. Vegetarianism is common among Hindu individuals. Hinduism involves the practice of Dharma, which refers in general to living the right way, or righteousness.

The spiritual teacher and psychologist Ram Dass, born as Richard Alpert, embraced Hinduism as a young man. He is known for his early work studying LSD and popularizing the phrase, "Be Here Now," which reflects the importance of awareness and being present moment to moment.

SIKIHISM

Sikhism is a religion founded in the 1400s in the Punjab region of India by Guru Nanak. "The word of Sikhi is commonly known as Gurmat which means "wisdom of the Guru." The principal belief is the concept of "oneness of God" where both one's secular life and spiritual life are blended as if one. Sikhs believe that all religious are equally valid and merely represent different perspectives concerned with the same object – an active, creative and practical life of truthfulness, fidelity, self-control and purity.

Sikh men are required to wear a Dastaar, a turban that covers the uncut hair on their head and signifies their spirituality. Sikhs have increasingly become vulnerable to hate crimes in the United States often due to being mistaken for "radical Muslims."

JUDAISM

Jewish ethnicity, nationally, and religion are strongly interrelated. Nearly two percent of the U.S. population identifies as Jewish. Judaism has four major aspects ranging from more progressive to more conservative: Reconstructionist, Reform, Conservative, and Orthodox. The mystical aspect of Judaism is based on the Kabballah, an esoteric and mystical teaching that began with Judaism and has more recently been popularized when combined with some Christian and New Age teachings.

 You can ask your client:

- *What role does being Jewish play in your life?*
- *In what ways is it important to you?*
- *How do you affirm your identity as a Jewish person in the U.S.?*

I Am A Cultural Jew

It is common that many people who identify as Jewish are not religious or spiritually Jewish. Thus one cannot assume anything upon introductions. I was raised in the conservative Jewish tradition, which is a patriarchal religion. On the one hand it emphasizes ethics and social justice, and yet on the other I have no doubt but that it contributed to the development of my feminism at an early age. Like many Jews (and unlike in many religions) I am a cultural Jew not a religious Jew. I do not adhere to any of the religious beliefs or traditions of Judaism, but I do value some of the ethical precepts, like Tikkun Olam-doing good in the world-and of course I enjoy Jewish food!

My Mother's Story

I will always remember this story my mother told me. She went to an all girls college and in 1944 traveled to New Hampshire with a group of girls. They entered the hotel where one of the girls had made reservations for their group, however when my mother went to check in she was told that they did not allow Jews in the hotel. Her name was a Jewish name. This was extremely traumatic for her, and affected her for the rest of life. As she sat with advanced dementia in her early 80s, this was among the very few stories she repeated about her life.

Did you know?

- *Tikkum Olam* = repairing the world or healing the world. It is one of the three great pillars of Judaism that requires acts of kindness and compassion, direct service to the community and philanthropy.

- A Jewish Buddhist (also called Jewbu or Jubu or Buju) is a person with a Jewish background who practices Buddhism, including meditation. A number of notable teachers of Buddhism, in particular Vipassana or mindfulness meditation in the United States are also Jewish by birth or practice. It is estimated that 30% of Western Buddhists are from Jewish heritage.

Haredi Judaism and Arranged Marriages

Like many religions, Judaism also has a strong conservative or fundamentalist sect called Orthodox Judaism.

Haredi Judaism is a type of Orthodox Judaism that values separation from modern secular culture. Haredi Judaism has often been referred to as "Ultra-Orthodox," however, those who live in such communities find this label to be highly offensive. There are about 1.5 million Haredim worldwide and about 500,000 in the U.S. (of the 5 million Jews in the United States). Most Haredim live in and around New York City. Arranged marriage is culturally normative and separation between men and women in public places is also enacted.

The stigma against mental illness and seeking mental health care is high in the Haredi community just as it is in many fundamentalist conservative communities. The most common problem for which Orthodox patients seek help is marital difficulties associated with the patriarchal structure of the relationship.

LATTER DAY SAINTS/MORMON

The Church of Latter Day Saints believes that the church is restoring the "original church" of Jesus Christ. Its informal name is the "Mormon Church." The U.S. based National Council of Churches ranks the Mormon Church as the fourth largest denomination in the United States. The churches' doctrine holds that the president of the church is a prophet and a seer who has direct communications with God. There are approximately 15 million members in the United States.

Mental Health and Mormons

Mormons often feel discriminated against by mainstream society. The top mental health issues for Mormons are depression, anxiety, trauma, masturbation, pornography, addiction, marriage, and divorce. Sexual intimacy, parenting, faith crisis and coping with same-sex attraction as a Mormon are also among top concerns.

Joan, who is Mormon, is a massage therapist in a chiropractic office. She sees a wide variety of people who come in for treatment. Many Mormon people come in for the variety of bodywork treatments to support their healing. Many bodywork therapies require some degree of disrobing.

Joan wants to let them know that she respects their modesty. She is mindful of the strong possibility that they will be wearing a type of undergarment that they promise to wear for the rest of their lives as a reminder of sacred covenants they have made with God. The garments are considered sacred, and are treated with respect, and usually tucked away where others won't see.

One client, Shelly, has requested treatment for her back, neck and shoulders, so she leaves her pants on. Joan tucks the sheets into her waistband so as not to make her garments oily and ask if it's all right to push them down a bit so as to expose the upper gluteal (buttock) muscle. The body is considered sacred, and the Mormon belief is that God requires modesty. Keeping covered as much as possible helps Shelly relax. Along with these measures, Joan keeps an open dialogue with her on the treatment plan so Shelly can choose what she wishes to receive for her massage/bodywork knowing that she may need to expose more skin than she is used to or feels comfortable with. Joan tells Shelly that she is in control of her modesty.

How would you feel working with Shelly?

_____

_____

Even if you are not providing medical care that requires disrobing, would you engage her adherence to her religious beliefs to support her physical and mental wellbeing? If so, how? If not, why not?

_____

_____

How would you deepen your knowledge of Shelly's background so that you could sensitively explore her concerns, develop rapport and gain her confidence?

_____

_____

NATIVE AMERICAN CHURCH

The Native American Church is a syncretic tradition incorporating elements of traditional native practices and Christianity, centered on the use of the peyote ritual. There are about 250,000 members of the church. Influenced by the ritual use of the peyote by the *Wixarrica* (Huichol) Indians of central west Mexico, the peyote is regarded as a sacred plant. Abstinence from alcohol is central to its tenets and participation is used extensively by individuals on the path of recovery from alcohol abuse.

The Native American Church is also known as the Peyote Religion. It combines cultural practices of southern U.S. and northern Mexico native peoples with elements of Christianity. In general, believers follow the peyote doctrine of one Supreme Being dealing with humans through different spirits. Peyote (a cactus nodule) is found primarily in north central Mexico. The Huichol and other peoples in Mexico use the cactus to induce supernatural visions and as medicine. The United States government banned the religion after it was organized in 1918 into the Native American Church, until the 1960s when followers organized a campaign to remove the U.S. government prohibitions.

ENTHEOGENS

Entheogens refer to 'God within us'—those plant substances that, when ingested, facilitate a divine experience. In the past, entheogens were commonly called hallucinogens, psychedelics, or psychotomimetics. Increasingly they are studied and applied in the clinical setting for the intractable symptoms of PTSD, including depression, hopelessness, anxiety and "loss of spirit."

- *What are your attitudes about the use of entheogens for mental health recovery?*
- *Would you refer a client? Why or why not?*
- *What do you know about entheogens? What would you like to find out?*

ATHEISM

Atheism is the absence of belief in any god or spiritual beings. Approximately 5% to 20% of the U.S. population identify as atheists. Many more men than women are atheists. People may be atheist, but consider themselves as spiritual, connected to a higher purpose or meaning, and also adhere to certain tenets of religion like Buddhism, Judaism, and Christianity. They may also believe in the teachings of religious figures like the Buddha and Jesus.

There does not appear to be a difference in mental health between people who are religious and those who are atheist. There is evidence of some hostility toward atheists and this may affect their mental and physical well-being. Atheists are considered "less acceptable" than other marginalized groups in the U.S., such as Muslims, homosexuals and recent immigrants. Since people who identify as atheists span all spectrum of identities in society, they may not be as easily recognizable.

ATHEISM

Directions: Please answer the following questions.

When you hear the word atheist, how do you react?

_____

_____

_____

_____

_____

If you believe in God, how would you feel working with a client who explicitly does not and is an activist in the atheist movement? How would you know if you need to refer this client to another clinician?

_____

_____

_____

_____

_____

Have you ever read any arguments for or against atheism? How might doing so affect your work with clients?

_____

_____

_____

_____

_____

SPIRITUALITY: DEEPENING A SENSE OF PURPOSE AND MEANING

In this chapter we have explored a selection of formal religions, belief systems and practices. I have also asked you to engage in reflection exercises that are designed to enhance our own competency as clinicians to be of service to our clients.

This final section provides some concepts and exercises that reflect practices adapted from specific cultures or spiritual practices, and reflect a more secular approach to deepening purpose and meaning in one's life. They are adaptable and accessible to all, whether one is deeply committed to a particular religion or an atheist. This allows us to engage in creative ways, to ask about and be present for the deep questions of life.

Generosity as Ritual

> *"Gentleness, self-sacrifice and generosity are the exclusive possession of no one race or religion."*
> — Mahatma Gandhi
> Father of the Indian Independence Movement

> *"Generosity is giving more than you can, and pride is taking less than you need."*
> — Khalil Gibran
> Lebanese-American Poet and Artist

Generosity is associated with spiritual and religious values, but also rooted in cultural values. In many ways generosity is the embodiment of spirit in action. Clinicians are by nature generous people. Generosity in this context refers not to giving material wealth, but to sharing the wealth of caring and compassion. Arthur W. Frank suggests, "medical generosity is the grace to welcome those who suffer."

Acts of generosity may be ritualized, such as gift giving at birthdays or volunteering each week, or they may be spontaneous acts of giving. Generosity in its highest form is both giving and receiving. The Dalai Lama, the spiritual leader of the Tibetan people suggests that generosity is the most natural outward expression of an inner attitude of compassion and loving-kindness. When one desires to alleviate the suffering of others and to promote their well-being, then generosity - in action, word, and thought - is this desire put into practice.

The intimate connection between generosity and cultures offers a fundamental demonstration of the importance of generosity to individual and collective wellbeing. Helping clients cultivate a generous spirit leads to increased compassion toward oneself and thus self-forgiveness and improved self-care.

GENEROSITY

Directions: Consider your experience of generosity and answer the following questions.

What role did generosity play in your early life? Who was generous? Who was not? Was generosity cultivated as a value to be enacted?

_____

_____

_____

_____

_____

In what ways was your family generous?

_____

_____

_____

_____

_____

In what ways selfish?

_____

_____

_____

_____

_____

What does your religion/spirituality/values say about generosity?

_____

_____

_____

_____

What role does generosity play in your current circle of friends and family?

_____

_____

_____

_____

_____

How do you respond to others who are more generous than you? Less generous than you?

_____

_____

_____

_____

_____

THE TRADITION OF POTLACH

The frequent practice of "gifting" is often said to reflect a "law of generosity." The biblical saying, "it is more blessed to give than to receive" speaks also to a psychological truth borne out by science. There are numerous health benefits to generosity and gratitude, it reduces stress, lowers blood pressure and improves mood. One of the most effective activities for people who are depressed or who have lost hope is to volunteer and serve others who are in need. To act generously is built into the fabric of tribal cultures across North America.

In this exercise, generosity is expressed by organizing a potlatch (give-away), which is ritual gifting in ceremony and at feasts. The common term: "potluck" comes from the term potlach.

This exercise is beneficial to anyone who undertakes it. It can be explored with a client at a specific stage of healing or can be done as an expression of gratitude and generosity. It may be done with a small or large group.

To create your potlach consider the setting and the purpose of the potlach. You may create it with friends, family, colleagues, or spiritual community. The potlach involves the gifting of goods and resources including food at a public gathering. The head of the group is most often responsible for acquiring and storing goods, which could be blankets, pots, carvings, fabrics, art pieces, food and other valuable items.

A spokesperson is identified to speak on behalf of the group that will give away the goods and items calling out the names of individuals who will receive the gifts. The spokesperson will call out the name of the recipients and perhaps name something special or important about their qualities, each in turn will rise to receive the gift, and then hold the gift aloft while loudly praising the givers. When all of the gifts have been given away, the family or group head of the givers will stand and thank all of those who participated and then later thank the spokesperson by lavishing praise and offering some goods or other form of wealth. Following the potlach a big meal is shared.

MEDITATION

One of the most important revolutions in mental health in the last 40 years has been the recognition of the role of meditation for mental and physical well-being and the inclusion of various models of contemplation drawn from the world's practices.

Meditation is practiced in many religions and cultural practices and is increasingly applied as an approach to stress reduction and self-regulation. While various forms of meditation may derive from specific religious practices, meditation as it is practiced for mental health may fit in with the client's existing belief system.

Meditation: Possible Side Effects

While meditation is safe and leads to mental and physical health benefits, there are times when it can become problematic for certain individuals. These are individuals who may not have a well-developed ego structure or who may be obsessive in their practices and can "overdose" on meditation. There is a saying, "Before you can lose your ego, you must attain it…you must have an ego in order to lose it." This refers to the importance of ensuring that the tool of meditation is applied appropriately with individuals. While meditation shows some benefit with people with psychosis and mania, too much meditation, can also precipitate depression mania in people with a previous history or no history of psychiatric disorders. Like all methods of self-care and healing, it must be aligned with the needs of the individual.

Different Types Meditation

There are 3 main types of meditation with many specific religious or cultural methods that combine various elements used in combinations. Some emphasize breath, or sound, inner or vocalized but most all are designed to facilitate quieting the mind and body.

Concentration Meditation — involves focusing on a sound a mantra or object.

Awareness Meditation — involves being aware moment to moment of what is happening

Mindfulness — combines both awareness and concentration.

Did you know?

In 1989, Salish communities in British Columbia and western Washington restored the "Canoe Journey" to ritually retrace the sea-going travels from village to village. For the last 20 years, upwards of 90 canoes with as many as 20 paddlers each, travel from their home village sites and converge on a pre-determined village host, after weeks of travel. The Canoe Journey and potlach have become central to the restoration of generosity practice. These traditions facilitate a transpersonal experience and meaning-making as it restores the health within communities ravaged by substance abuse, depression and trauma, all of which can be understood to derive from loss of community and cultural coherence.

The Canoe Journey is a five-day celebratory and healing ritual open to the public that is held annually and hosted by a different tribal community each year in the Pacific Northwest and Canada. Each year upwards of 5,000 people gather to welcome canoe families who have traveled many miles over open sea to reach their host's welcome. Paddlers, healers and visitors alike share in food, gifts and community exchange during this celebration of culture, sobriety and gifting.

MEDITATION AND MENTAL WELL-BEING CLIENT EXERCISE

An ancient yogic wisdom suggests that to control the breath is to control the mind.

Directions: Before introducing this exercise, I discuss with the client their experience in meditation or prayer, and ascertain if they perceive any obstacles to meditating. When working with clients who are anxious or stressed, I suggest that we spend the first few minutes of a session relaxing, breathing, and meditating. There are numerous methods and knowing several will allow you tailor this practice to the needs of each client.

- At the beginning of each clinical session, spend five minutes practicing breath mindfulness.

- Sitting comfortably balanced, gently rest hands on the knees, keeping the elbows close to the body.

- Begin by following the natural rhythm of the breath then deepen/lengthen the inhalation and exhalation, keeping the lengths of the inhalations and exhalations relatively even. A good rhythm to begin with is a four-count rhythm.

- Allow the breath to find its own rhythm and then as comfort increases count to four during the inhalation, hold to a count of four, exhale to a count of four, and then hold to a count of four.

- Do not be concerned if the count shifts.

LOVING KINDNESS MEDITATION

Metta bhavana, or loving-kindness meditation, is an exercise about developing compassion and love. It comes from the Buddhist tradition, but it can be adapted and practiced by anyone. I have shared it with clients who are feeling the pain of a broken heart and who have themselves "lost heart." It may also be used to stop the obsessive, repetitive fears and worries that often plague a traumatized or depressed person.

Directions: While individuals are saying these lines silently, they may envision their hearts and create images that offer healing.

> *May I be filled with loving-kindness*
>
> *May I be well*
>
> *May I be peaceful and at ease*
>
> *May I be happy*

LABYRINTHS AND WALKING MEDITATION

While you may not embark on a long pilgrimage you might choose to journey through a labyrinth. Labyrinths are a type of walking mandala or walking meditation. They are designed to bring alignment and self-regulation and may lead to a transcendent experience. A labyrinth is a winding pattern whose single path leads to a center and leads out again the same way. Labyrinths are commonly thought of in the context of the Christian tradition though date to pre-Christian times and are found in many of the world's religions, including Wicca. Therapists can help their clients work through problems and attain clarity and inner peace with labyrinth walking.

Labyrinth walking as a form of meditation enhances psychological and spiritual growth by integrating kinesthetic and introspective awareness. As an embodied metaphorical journey or pilgrimage, the labyrinth is a symbol of transformation. Walking the labyrinth has three phases. In the journey toward the center, the walker focuses on a particular question or issue. Once the center is reached, the individual asks for an insight or image to help in understanding the issue. On the way out she/he concentrates on a question such as "how will I know that I am on the right path.

Labyrinth walking can be used in conjunction with other psychotherapeutic methods and used in settings as diverse as transpersonal therapy, spiritual retreats, and as a therapeutic approach for children, adults in transition and people with dementia.

In my clinical practice I use labyrinth walking as a ritual to signify the completion of a stage of recovery or as an activity to initiate a new phase, direction or focus— for example following a graduation or getting divorced or for those facing an "empty nest" or retirement.

Find a labyrinth in your area and walk it.
Access the Labyrinth Locator and find labyrinth locations around the globe. http://labyrinthlocator.com/

Labyrinth coloring books are a meditative approach to art in the office. Ask a client to color a labyrinth of their choice.

NEW AGE

The term "New Age emerged during the 1960's and refers to a syncretic amalgamation of a variety of spiritual beliefs and practices." Many influences are drawn from holistic philosophies, ancient wisdoms, theosophy, eastern religions, and American Indian traditions. It incorporates esoteric practices, which may include channeling, intentionality, paganism, and cosmic beliefs about the human place in the universe. No single "version" of New Age exists, but the practices, networks, and beliefs and constituted a significant force among North American religious practices.

New Age Mental Health Methods

One of the more common methods of healing for mental health among "new age" adherents is shamanism or neo-shamanism. Shamanic healing often refers to techniques of ecstasy that facilitate neurobiological attachment. This in turn leads to brain synchrony and cohesion among ritual participants.

The shaman is the "wounded healer" who facilitates a journey via altered states of consciousness as a road to self-discovery and healing. Counseling and psychotherapy is, in some respects, modern shamanic practice that reestablishes connection to self and others.

Core shamanism or "soul retrieval" is a psychotherapeutic practice that facilitates the retrieval of a lost aspect of self (or soul) in order to restructure identity. These mind-body-spirit activities may include trance dance, drumming ceremonies, fire walking, vision quests, and entheogenic-facilitated experiences. These practices support individual and group contact with the divine.

Spirituality and the Arts

The arts may be used to express deeper meaning, purpose and spirituality. The following exercises can be done with an individual client or with a group and tailored to the developmental needs of people of all ages.

Sacred Journeys

Pilgrimages are often undertaken for a spiritual quest, to engage the sacred and divine in time and space and to reach a destination. They may involve a solitary journey or one with family or large groups. Many people engage in a pilgrimage not of their own religion but to partake in the spiritual aspect of engaging the divine. Still others undertake a "walking meditation" to find a way within, exploring the way on foot. Others undertake arduous journeys to test their faith as in Cheryl Strayed's book (and movie), *Wild*.

Examples of Pilgrimages

The Way of St. James to Santiago de Compostela, Spain Pilgrimage — A well-known walking pilgrimage undertaken by people of all faiths is the Camino de Santiago. It is a UNESCO world heritage site that is network of ancient routes of about 500 miles across Europe, in particular France and Spain.

Hajj. The pilgrimage to Mecca — The pilgrimage of Muslims is an annual event to the city of Mecca in Saudi Arabia. Nearly 2 million people participate in this ritual which is considered both obligatory at least once in a lifetime as well as a spiritual renewal.

Procession of Regla — Every year devoted Cubans meet in Regla to honor the Catholic "Afro Cuban" virgin, Yemayá.

Osun-Osgobo — The annual ritual festival of Osun-Osgobo celebrates Osun the goddess oif fetility in the African Yoriuba tradition

Skikoku Pilgrimage — A 750 mile pilgrimage of 200,000 Japanese Buddhists occurs throughout the year in Japan.

> • *What are some examples of pilgrimages?* • *Have you ever been on a pilgrimage?*
> • *Might you recommend a client undertake a pilgrimage?*

INNER JOURNEY/OUTER JOURNEY

What kind of journey are you called to do?

_____

_____

What is the meaning of homeland for your spirit, for your religion?

_____

_____

_____

What are some examples of pilgrimages that you resonate with?

_____

_____

_____

_____

Have you ever been on a pilgrimage? If not where might you go? Take some time to explore your options, including groups that organize these spirit-adventures.

_____

_____

_____

Might you recommend a client undertake a pilgrimage and if so why?

_____

_____

_____

_____

CREATING A MANDALA

Mandala (Sanskrit: 'circle') is a spiritual and ritual symbol in Hinduism and Buddhism. It represents the universe and is usually a geometric multicolored pattern. I use mandalas, or mandala coloring books, with clients for many reasons. It can be a meditative and creative activity which helps people relax and focus. It is also an opportunity to talk while creating art. It is especially helpful with children and adolescents who may be hesitant to talk.

You can print this off at go.pesi.com/multicultural and you or your clients can color it in and enjoy the creative experience.

SPIRIT COLLAGE

Spirit collages may be adapted to the needs of the client for personal empowerment or spiritual and religious growth and expression. It is an arts-based approach to reflect on different aspects of the self. Both religious and non-religious individuals can do this exercise. It focuses on creating images that reflect inner sense of self and purpose and wellbeing.

Directions: Gather magazines and other craft materials that are image-rich. Consider items from nature: feathers, leaves, twigs, rocks small gems, anything that you want to become part of your collage.

Now make a list of words or phrases of times of your life you wish to represent. You may wish to identify:

• Birth or envision your passing

_____

• Motherhood or fatherhood

_____

• List people: an ancestor, spouse, parent, sibling, a beloved animal friend

_____

• List places you have lived or would like to live

_____

• List spirit qualities you embody or would like to emphasize: joy, presence, authenticity

_____

Place these words on cards and incorporate into your collage to reflect visually what these words mean to you.

SOUND AND SPIRIT

In mental health we use music in a variety of ways. We encourage clients to sing, make music, or listen to music. We don't often chant with our clients. Chanting is the saying or singing of sounds or songs individually or in a group, and is most often associated with spiritual or religious devotion.

Making sounds, singing and chanting transports the soul and heals the body and mind. Singing improves breathing and is relaxing, and allows for verbal and sound expression when words fall short. Singing can be a transcendent experience and may be associated with a transpersonal experience or lead to deep relaxation and a sense of creative expression.

Singing, chanting and making sounds can self-regulate the psychobiology of the brain, body and states of consciousness. Singing in local community groups can help to reduce loneliness and provide nonverbal ways of expressing feelings.

Toning is a form of singing that focuses on making sounds, often using vowels as extended notes. Toning does not require the ability to sing, but does involve making sounds that create vibrations, which can be directed toward pain, discomfort, or unpleasant emotions in areas of the body.

THE RITUAL OF TONING SOUNDS

Directions: Toning involves making sounds based on the vowels. First, you inhale and then on the exhale makes a vowel sound for the length of the breath; with just a pause to inhale, you exhale again, repeating the sound.

This may be repeated several times. You can experiment with different sound and vowels. Toning sounds include Ohhhhhh . . . Ahhhhhhh . . . Eeeeeee . . . Iiiiiiiiiiiii, and Uuuuuuuuuu.

When I work with clients who have pain or physical discomfort, I ask them to place their hand on the area that is painful and then to tone until they feel the vibration on that area or it feels like the right sound to relieve that pain. Once they identify the sound I match it by toning the same tone with them. We do this several times and then move to another area of the body.

EXPLORING YOUR NEXT STEPS WITH RELIGION AND SPIRITUALITY

Directions: Think about the following questions.

• *What are your next steps for exploring the role of spirituality and religion in your work with clients?*

• *Can you think of clients with whom you may explore spirituality?*

• *Are there clients with whom you have discussed this topic but now might do so with specific exercises?*

• *Are there additional books, or trainings you wish to undertake to deepen your own integration of spirituality into your work as a professional?*

RESOURCES

Books and Publications

Adams Media. (2014.) *The Big Book of Mandalas Coloring Book: More Than 200 Mandala Coloring Pages for Inner Peace and Inspiration.* Fort Collins, CO: Adams Media.

Eason, A.,Colmant, S., & Winterowd, C. (2009). Sweat therapy theory, practice, and efficacy. *Journal of Experiential Education, 32*(2), 121-136.

Feldman, D. Story about Debbie Feldman, the author of *Unorthodox: the Scandalous Rejection of My Hasidic Roots*
http://abcnews.go.com/Health/hasidic-jew-runs-orthodox-roots-arranged-marriage-child/story?id=15540395

Haas, M. (2013). *Dakini Power: Twelve Extraordinary Women Shaping the Transmission of Tibetan Buddhism in the West.* Ithaca, New York: Snow Lion Publications.

Jervis, L. J., & AI-SUPERPFP Team. *Di.* Disillusionment, Faith, and Cultural Traumatization on a Northern Plains Reservation.Traumatology March 2009 15: 11-22.

McArdle, T. (2014). *Day of the Dead Coloring Book.* East Petersburg: Design Originals

McArdle, T. (2014). *Nature Mandalas Coloring Book.* East Petersburg: Design Originals

Pargament, K. I. (2007). *Spiritually Integrated Psychotherapy: Understanding and Addressing the Sacred.* New York, New York: Guilford Press.

Pargament, K. I. (Ed.). (2013). *APA Handbook of Psychology, Religion, and Spirituality.* Washington, D.C. American Psychological Association

Rassool, G. H. (Ed.). (2014). *Cultural Competence in Caring for Muslim Patients* (Kindle Edition), Palgrave MacMillan.

Robert, Tracey E, Kelly, Virginia. (2014) *Critical Incidents in Integrating Spirituality Into Counseling.* Alexandria, Virginia: American Counseling Association

Thomas, Debie: A First-person Account. *My Parents Chose My Husband*
http://www.slate.com/articles/life/family/2013/08/arranged_marriage_in_america_my_parents_moved_here_from_india_raised_me.html

Wilson, J. P. (1989). *Trauma, Transformation, and Healing: An Integrative Approach to Theory, Research, and Post-Traumatic Therapy.* New York, New York: Routledge

Winston, H. (2005). *Unchosen: The Hidden Lives of Hasidic Rebels* Boston, Massachusetts: Beacon Press.

To learn more about Buddhist teachers have applied Buddhist teachings for the treatment of mental illness
Thích Nhât Hanh is a Vietnamese Zen Buddhist monk, teacher, author, poet and peace activist known for his work in helping veterans from the Viet Nam war find peace within.
No Mud, No Lotus: The Art of Transforming Suffering, by Thích Nhât Hanh, 2014.
The Pocket Thích Nhât Hanh, Shambhala Pocket Classics, 2012.
American born Pema Chödrön is an ordained nun and Buddhist teacher.
When Things Fall Apart: Heart Advice for Difficult Times, by Pema Chödrön, an ordained nun and Buddhist teacher.

To Learn More about Labyrinths
Aliyah Schick. Labyrinths: Meditative Coloring Book 5: Adult Coloring for relaxation, stress reduction, meditation, spiritual connection, prayer, centering, healing, into your deep true self; for ages 9-109 2011 Sacred Imprints http://meditativecoloring.com/labyrinths/
Lauren Artress, Walking a Sacred Path: Rediscovering the Labyrinth as a Spiritual Practice 2006 Riverhead Books
Dakini Power: Twelve Extraordinary Women Shaping the Transmission of Tibetan Buddhism in the West, by Michaela Haas, 2013. Ithaca, New York: Snow Lion Publications
Sacred Journeys. PBS documentary about six sacred journeys with Bruce Feiler
http://www.pbs.org/wgbh/sacredjourneys/content/home/

To read more on the roots of generosity across cultures and religions
http://generosityresearch.nd.edu/more-about-the-initiative/what-is-generosity/
http://learningtogive.org/resources/folktales/guide.asp

Movies/Videos
Fill the Void
This film by Rama Burshtein follows the lives of an Orthodox Hasidic family living in Tel-Aviv as they deal with trauma and make difficult life decisions.
For more about Ignacio Martín-Baró view this video:
http://www.bc.edu/centers/humanrights/Videos/lykes.html

Islam's Reformation
In a probing and personal conversation, Reza Aslan opens a refreshing window on religion in the world and Islam in particular.
http://onbeing.org/program/reza-aslan-on-islams-reformation/7039
Standing on Sacred Ground
A film about eight indigenous cultures around the world taking a stand against industrial mega-projects, consumer culture, resource extraction, competing religions, tourists and climate change.
http://standingonsacredground.bullfrogcommunities.com/ssg_about

The Way
The actor Martin Sheen stars in this fictional movie about spiritual pilgrimage on the "Camino: "The Way of St. James." Available on Netflix.
Voices of the West Bank and Israel
https://vimeo.com/81459973
Walking the Camino: Six Ways to Santiago

This documentary is about "The Camino" a world-renowned, UNESCO World Heritage Site declared as first European Cultural Itinerary. This 500 mile walking pilgrimage to the city of Santiago de Compostela is undertaken by thousands of people annually.
http://caminodocumentary.org
Mormon Stories Podcast
Exploring celebrating and challenging Mormon culture through stories
http://mormonstories.org/about/

Mormons in Popular Culture
Big Love, a fictional TV Series on HBO
The Book of Mormon, a musical satire

Music
Coming Home - Eyal Rivlin, Danya Uriel, a.k.a. Temple
"Our music is a carrier wave, a sonic container for prayer."
https://www.youtube.com/watch?v=2zrPFxxT1VM

Organizations
American Association of Christian Counselors
http://www.aacc.net/
National Christian Counselors Association (NCCA)
American Association of Christian Therapists (AACT)
International Christian Counselors Alliance (ICCA)
International Association of Christian Counseling Professionals (IACCP)
Board of Christian Professional and Pastoral Counselors (BCPPC)
Association for Spiritual, Ethical and Religious Values in Counseling Competencies.
The Association for Transpersonal Psychology
http://www.atpweb.org/about.aspx
Nefesh, the International Network of Orthodox Mental Health Professionals
https://www.nefesh.org/
Unchained at Last
An organization that provides legal support and financial aid to women in arranged marriages from several cultures throughout the United States. www.unchainedatlast.org

MAPS
Multidisciplinary Association for Psychedelic studies
Academic and clinical research on the role of entheogens and medical marijuana for mental health including drug addiction PTSD and palliative care.
http://www.maps.org/

Web Resources
American Atheists
http://atheists.org/
Explore Sacred Lands
Interactive map of sacred land sites throughout the world. Identify where your peoples are from.
http://www.sacredland.org/home/resources/sacred-lands-interactive-map/

Journal of Muslim Mental Health
http://www.journalofmuslimmentalhealth.org/
Mormon Mental Health
http://www.mormonmentalhealth.org/
In the Light of Reverence
In the Light of Reverence explores American culture's relationship to nature in three places considered sacred by native peoples: the Colorado Plateau in the Southwest, Mount Shasta in California, and Devils Tower in Wyoming.
http://www.sacredland.org/in-the-light-of-reverence/#sthash.aXFlgsYq.dpuf
NKI Center of Excellence in Culturally Competent Mental Health
http://ssrdqst.rfmh.org/cecc/index.php?q=node/25
Tikkun
Tikkun magazine brings together progressive Jewish, Christian, Muslim, Hindu, Buddhist, Wiccan, secular humanist, and agnostic/atheist voices to talk about social transformation and strategies for political and economic democratization.
http://www.tikkun.org/nextgen/

Chapter 6

Gender, Sex and Sexual Orientation

Chapter 6
Gender, Sex and Sexual Orientation

*"Gay marriage will be universally accepted in time. But if I may be so bold
as to say to gays and lesbians, don't wait for that time to arrive. Just as my father
and his generation did not 'wait' for their civil rights, nor should you.
The toothpaste ain't going back in the tube. The tide has turned."*

— John Ridley, Screenwriter

Gender, sexuality, and sexual orientation make up a complex spectrum of identities, behaviors and sexual partner attractions. There are a growing number of terms and expressions of gender and sexuality and these terms change and evolve as popular awareness and inter-social contact increases.

As with our discussions of cultural, ethnic and religious identities, what matters most is how individuals self-identify—what they prefer to be called by their friends and by the surrounding society. One should never assume another person's identity based on appearance, since to do so will usually inaccurately identify who that person actually is. It is always best to ask people how they identify, including what pronouns they prefer.

Gender and sex are different. Biological sex occurs along a spectrum and is assigned at birth according to the physical structure of the reproductive organs, and is defined by chromosomes, hormones, and genitalia. There are more than two sets of possibilities, biological sex is a spectrum of possibilities.

Gender is a social construct that may vary from culture to culture. Each of us engages in *gender expression*. This refers to the myriad ways in which we reflect our masculinity or femininity. This can change throughout the day by the clothing we wear to work and wear at home, or when we go out with some friends or not others

Did you know?
• Estimates range from 1.6 to 3.7% of the population identifying as gay or lesbian with 0.7 to 1.8 % identifying as bisexual.
• The largest gay and lesbian populations in the U.S. as percentage of the population live in Hawaii (5%), Oregon (4.9%), California (4%), Texas (3.6%), and Massachusetts (3.4%).
• Cities with highest percentage of gays and lesbians: San Francisco, Seattle, Atlanta, Minneapolis, and Boston.
• 21% of LGBT youth reported being physically assaulted at school and 92% reported having been verbally abused.
• Nearly one in six transgender Americans has been to prison. Nearly half of all black transgender people have been in prison.

for example. Some people are more *gender-expansive* than others. This means that they expand the definition of gender beyond stereotypical norms through their own expression. What is considered gender-expansive in one epoch may become gender-normative in another. Consider when men began wearing long hair in the 1960's and the uproar that followed; today it goes unnoticed.

Effective mental and physical health services delivery depends upon developing our awareness and sensitivity about gender identity and sexual orientation. Many mental health and religious concepts of gender and sexual orientation can harm individuals. Discovering our own attitudes and educating ourselves is requisite for working with all individuals.

HEALTH AND HEALTHCARE IN LESBIAN, GAY, BISEXUAL, AND TRANSGENDER COMMUNITIES

While strides are being made in social acceptance of lesbian, gay, bisexual, and transgender (LGBT) communities, there are still significant disparities in their overall health and access to healthcare, especially compared to their heterosexual counterparts. The HIV epidemic remains the most serious problem among gay and bisexual men, who account for two-thirds of new infections. Among transgender women, more than 28% are HIV positive.

Stigma, and discrimination in the workplace exacerbate these problems. These can lead to substandard care and, in some cases, the denial of care due to gender and sexual identity. Other factors include gaps in healthcare coverage, lack of affordable care, and discrimination by health providers. Additionally, although laws prohibit hospitals and long-term care facilities from denying visitation to same-sex partners, they are unevenly implemented. In most states there are no laws prohibiting the firing of LGBT people based on their sexual orientation, which can abruptly end health insurance coverage. Nor do federal regulations prohibit discrimination based on sexual orientation outside of state marketplaces.

ATTITUDES ABOUT GAY AND LESBIAN

Directions: Please fill out the worksheet.

If you close your eyes and allow your stream of consciousness to flow, what are the first words that rise to your awareness when you think of:

Gay Males	Lesbian Women	Gay Boys	Lesbian Girls
_____	_____	_____	_____
_____	_____	_____	_____
_____	_____	_____	_____
_____	_____	_____	_____
_____	_____	_____	_____

Do you use the term "lesbian/gay" or "homosexual"? What do these terms mean to you? Do you wonder which is "correct"?

_____

_____

_____

Is there someone close to you who identifies as lesbian/gay? A friend? A family member?

_____

_____

_____

Do you have coworkers who identify as lesbian/gay? An employer? Employees? How would you describe your relationship?

_____

_____

_____

How do you feel about lesbian and gay parenting?

_____

_____

_____

Where do those beliefs come from?

_____

_____

_____

How do you feel about lesbian and gay adoptions?

_____

_____

_____

Where do those beliefs come from?

_____

_____

_____

Do your current beliefs differ from the beliefs you grew up with? If so, in what ways?

_____

_____

Sometimes clinicians feel a conflict between their religious values that are anti-LGBT and their clinical training. Is this something that you struggle with?

_____

_____

What might be the next steps toward a resolution? Who can be a resource to you?

_____

_____

CASE VIGNETTE: LESBIAN PARENTS

Directions: Please fill out the worksheet.

Marie and Joan have been together four years. They were referred to you by a straight couple whom you had helped during their two years of infertility. Marie and Joan are seeking counseling because Marie wants to become pregnant using the sperm of Joan's brother. You are uncomfortable with lesbians raising children and are not sure whether you should continue to work with Marie and Joan or to refer them elsewhere.

How do you respond?

_____

_____

What might you do to deepen your knowledge of lesbian parenting and pregnancy so that you could sensitively explore these concerns, develop rapport and gain their confidence?

_____

_____

Or will you recuse yourself from treating Joan and Marie?

_____

_____

Will you benefit from counseling? Supervision or further education?

_____

_____

Is this an example of the need to overcome your own bias? Is this possible for you at this time?

_____

_____

LGBT TERMS

LGBTQA — Acronym for lesbian, gay, bisexual, transgender, questioning and allies. Although all of the different identities within "LGBT" are often lumped together (and share sexism as a common root of oppression), there are specific health and social needs and concerns related to each individual identity.

Coming Out — This is the process of acknowledging one's sexual orientation and gender identity to other people. For most LGBT people this is a lifelong process.

Gay — A person who is attracted primarily to members of the same sex. Although it can be used for any sex (e.g., gay man, gay woman, gay person), "lesbian" is sometimes the preferred term for women who are attracted to women.

Gender Dysphoria — A person's experienced gender does not match their gender at birth. A person with gender dysphoria may feel and experience the world as the other gender, and may also desire to be treated as the other gender or change their sexual characteristics. (Source: http://www.dsm5.org)

> ### Did you know?
>
> Religious Attitudes and The LGBTQ Community
>
> - Between 2006 and 2012, the number of congregations allowing an openly gay or lesbian couple to become full-fledged members grew from 37% to 48%.
>
> - The number of congregations that allowed openly gay and lesbian members to assume any lay leadership position also increased – from 18% in 2006 to 26% in 2012.
>
> - Between 2006 and 2014, acceptance of same-sex marriage among the general public grew from 35% to about 50%.

Gender Fluidity — A gender expression that changes, sometimes from day to day. Gender fluid children are not defined by any specific gender and may identify as a boy one day and a girl the next, with different behaviors and interests. (Source:https://www.genderspectrum.org/quick-links/understanding-gender/)

Queer — (1) An umbrella term sometimes used by LGBTQA people to refer to the entire LGBT community. (2) The word queer is an in-group term, but can be considered offensive to some people, depending on their generation, geographic location and relationship with the word.

Genderqueer — Genderqueer people self-identify outside of the widely accepted sexual binary (i.e. "men" and "women"). Genderqueer may also refer to people who identify as both transgender AND queer, i.e. individuals who challenge both gender and sexuality conventions and see gender identity and sexual orientation as overlapping and interconnected.

Heterosexist — Heterosexuals who are prejudiced against people who are homosexual and bisexual, with the belief that heterosexuality is the only normal sexual orientation. Heterosexism was central to mental and physical health tenets until recently and remains present in many religions.

Straight — A person who is only attracted to members of the opposite sex, also known as heterosexual.

Homophobia — A range of negative attitudes and feelings toward homosexuality or people who are identified or perceived as being lesbian, gay, bisexual or transgender (LGBT).

Homosexual — A clinical term for people who are attracted to members of the same sex. Some people find this term offensive.

Internalized Phobias — LGBT people may internalize negative beliefs of homophobia, lesbian phobia, bi-phobia, and transphobia.

Intersex — A person whose sexual anatomy or chromosomes do not fit with the traditional markers of "female" and "male." For example: people born with both female and male anatomy (penis, testicles, vagina, uterus) or people born with XXY chromosomes. There are many variations of biological sex and these variations occur in approximately every 1 in 1500 infants.

In the Closet — Describes a person who keeps their sexual orientation or gender identity a secret from some or all people.

Lesbian — A woman who is primarily attracted to other women.

Questioning — For some, the process of exploring and discovering one's own sexual orientation, gender identity, or gender expression.

Pansexual — A person who experiences sexual, romantic, physical, and spiritual attraction for members of all gender identities/expressions, not just people who fit into the standard gender binary (i.e. men and women).

Polyamory — From the root words *poly*, meaning many, and *amor*, meaning love, polyamory means "many loves." It refers to multipartner relationships that are non-possessive, ethical, honest, and responsible. It is an alternative to the social norm of monogamy. http://www.polyamorysociety.org/page6.html)

Sexual Orientation — The type of sexual, romantic, and physical attraction someone feels toward others.

Transgender — This term has many definitions. It is frequently used as an umbrella term to refer to all people who do not identify with their assigned gender at birth or the binary gender system. This includes transsexuals, cross-dressers, gender queer, drag kings, drag queens, two-spirit people, and others. Some transgender people feel they exist not within one of the two standard gender categories, but rather somewhere between, beyond, or outside of those two genders.

Transphobia — The fear or hatred of transgender people or gender non-conforming behavior. Like biphobia, transphobia can also exist among lesbian, gay, and bisexual people, as well as among heterosexual people.

Transsexual — A person whose gender identity is different from their biological sex, who may undergo medical treatments to change their biological sex, often times to align it with their gender identity, or they may live their lives as another sex.

(Source: http://internationalspectrum.umich.edu/life/definitions)

TRANSGENDER INDIVIDUALS

"I am transgender. I was born male and identify as female.
But I like to say that I'm a girl stuck in a boy's body. I transitioned when I was
6 or 7 to more of a girl. And now I'm— well, almost completely female."

— Lia Hegarty, age 9

"My given name was Naima, and now my name is Daniel. I've been a boy for three years.
And I've been— I was a girl for six. I don't like to be called a "she" anymore, and I just— I
really like it that they think of me as a—as a boy. I think it's hard to get used to it because I
was a girl for so long, and I haven't been a boy for a very long time."

— Daniel Heuman, age 9

The quotes above are from the documentary "Growing up Trans" Frontline on PBS.

Transgender individuals are generally defined as people who feel and experience a different gender identity than the biological sex they were born with.

Clinicians may contribute to the well-being of transgender individuals at any stage of life including evaluating children for hormone use at or after puberty or evaluating children and adults for sex reassignment surgery. Surgeons in the U.S. usually require letters from mental health clinicians, attesting to the mental health of the individual who wishes to undergo sex reassignment surgery. Clinicians may also be called upon to support and educate parents and siblings of transgender children.

Many children become aware at a very young age that they are trans. Increasingly clinicians are working with parents and their children to support their child socially, developmentally, and medically.

Transgender children and adults can experience a variety of mental health challenges including gender dysphoria, depression, anxiety, isolation, bullying, and rejection by family and friends. As children become adolescents, puberty brings an onslaught of challenges as hormones start creating unwanted changes.

Transitioning

"Transitioning" refers to changing ones external physical characteristics to conform to the inner felt sense of self as the opposite sex. It may include sex reassignment options that occur along a spectrum, ranging from hormones, laser hair removal, voice lessons, to a range of surgeries including cosmetic surgery, (e.g., shaving of Adam's apple or breast implants, features refinement) to changing of sexual organs.

Each stage of development and growth may bring new decisions in identity, and transitioning may be a lifelong process. Of particular concern for clinicians is that medical procedures including hormones and sex reassignment surgeries are expensive and inaccessible to many clients.

Identity: Transracialism and Transgenderism

In June of 2015, a firestorm of controversy was ignited when Rachael Dolezal, an African Studies lecturer at Eastern Washington University and president of the Spokane chapter of the NAACP, was questioned about her ethnicity. The controversy swirled around her claims to blackness despite the testimony of her estranged Anglo parents who asserted that she has no black ancestry. Dolezal claimed that race and ethnicity are "multi-layered issues" that most people don't understand. This is an argument that emphasizes academics' contentions of the socially-constructed nature of race.

Dolezal's story lit up the blogosphere and social media, instigating contentious debates about "transracialism." It also sparked debates about whether or not the transracialism as articulated by Dolezal is comparable to transgenderism. Around the same time, U.S. Olympian Bruce Jenner, transitioned publicly to Caitlyn Jenner.

At their core, both issues center around how identity development is informed by elements such as race and gender. Transgenderism describes people whose identity does not unambiguously conform to their gender. Transgender individuals often explain that it is not a matter of choice. "Transracial" literally refers to the crossing of racial boundaries. The academic literature on transracialism applies the term "transracial" to adoption practices, describing the adoption of black children by white parents, thus focusing on issues of identity formation in children from transracial families. But the Dolezal story brought to light another way that the term "transracial" is being popularly used to describe people who assume an ethnic or racial identity which they were not born into. Little research exists on transracialism.

The heated debates raised more questions than they answered: in what ways is transracialism analogous to transgenderism? Where does the comparison fail? Can ethnic switching be viewed as arising from body dystopia in the same way transgendered people experience it? We accept people who "convert" to religions they were not born into. Why are we less likely to accept people who claim identities, especially identities of color, they are not born into?

TRANSRACIALISM AND TRANSGENDERISM

Directions: Please fill out the worksheet.

Do you know anyone who has changed their ethnic or gender identity?

_____

_____

_____

_____

_____

What kinds of images or internal dialogue come up for you about identity switching? Do you see distinctions between ethnic and gender switching?

_____

_____

_____

_____

_____

_____

What kinds of messages did you grow up with regarding ethnic and gender identity? Was identity solid and fixed or was it fluid and permeable? Have your views changed, and if so, how? What has influenced your thinking?

_____

_____

_____

_____

GENDER BIAS

Gender Bias — Refers to unequal treatment of women that occurs throughout all levels of society including employment, salary, health care, education, entertainment, and the media.

Distinguished gender law professor Joan Williams and her daughter, law student Rachel Dempsey, have identified four types of bias women encounter at work

1. Prove It Again: Women are forced to demonstrate their worth over and over.

2. Tightrope: Women have to navigate the path between being "too masculine" and "too feminine." They suggest this spectrum of pressure also varies across ethnicities, for example, Latinas who feel they must dress differently to avoid stereotyping.

3. Maternal Wall: The discrimination women face when they have children, especially in regard to hours, time off, and provision of child care.

4. Tug of War: When the strategies they employ for succeeding in a sexist workplace can pit them against each other. They noted variations of "in-fighting" among women across ethnicities, with African American women being less critical of older female colleagues than white women.

GENDER BIAS IN THE WORKPLACE

Directions: Please answer the following questions.

Have you experienced any of these forms of workplace bias?

_____

_____

_____

_____

What did you do about it?

_____

_____

_____

_____

Did/do you have any allies in the workplace?

_____

_____

_____

_____

Have you observed workplace bias against your colleagues? How did you feel about it? Were you able to act as an ally?

_____

_____

_____

_____

_____

RESOURCES

Access many of these resources online at www.healthalt.org

Books and Publications
Journal of Gay & Lesbian Mental Health

Kailey, M. (2006) *Just Add Hormones*. Boston, Massachusetts: Beacon Press.

Ryan, C. & Futterman, D. (1998). *Lesbian & Gay Youth: Care & Counseling*. New York: Columbia. University Press.

Movies/Videos
A Path Appears
Reporters, actors and advocates travel throughout the United States as they uncover the harshest forms of gender-based oppression and human rights violations, as well as the effective solutions being implemented to combat them.
http://apathappears.org/film/

PBS NewsHour Weekend's Stephen Fee reports on domestic violence on American Indian Reservations.
http://www.pbs.org/newshour/bb/law-uneven-justice-seen-reservations-victims-domestic-violence/

TransParent
TransParent is an American comedy-drama television series about a middle-aged father who comes out as trans to his family. It was created and directed by Jill Soloway based on some of her own family experiences.

Growing up Trans
Frontline documentary on PBS http://www.pbs.org/wgbh/pages/frontline/growing-up-trans/

Organizations

The Faith Trust Institute—a national, multi-faith, multicultural training and education organization with global reach working to end sexual and domestic violence. *A Perspective on Domestic Violence in the Muslim Community*.
http://www.faithtrustinstitute.org/resources/articles/DV-in-Muslim-Community.pdf

Family Acceptance Project
A research, intervention, education and policy initiative that works to prevent health and mental health risks for lesbian, gay, bisexual and transgender (LGBT) children and youth.
http://familyproject.sfsu.edu/

Web Resources
Standards of care document for the health of transsexual, transgender, and gender nonconforming people is available in multiple languages at the World Professional Association for Transgender Health. http://www.wpath.org/site_page.cfm?pk_association_webpage_menu=1351

Ban Bossy Movement
When a little boy asserts himself, he's called a "leader." Yet when a little girl does the same, she risks being branded "bossy." Words like bossy send a message: don't raise your hand or speak up. By middle school, girls are less interested in leading than boys—a trend that continues into adulthood. Together we can encourage girls to lead.
http://banbossy.com/

Gender Bias Learning Project: A Zany Brainy Look at a Serious Subject
The Center for WorkLife Law, with support from a NSF ADVANCE leadership grant, has developed this on-line gender bias training that teaches you to identify the four basic patterns of gender bias.
http://www.genderbiasbingo.com/

Power and Control Wheel
To better recognize the special needs and concerns of immigrant and refugee domestic violence survivors, the Minnesota Center Against Violence and Abuse at the University of Minnesota have created a specialized Power and Control Wheel.
http://www.bcbsm.com/pdf/DV_ReferenceGuide.pdf

Chapter 7
Abilities, Disabilities and the Body

Chapter 7
Abilities, Disabilities and the Body

*"Part of the problem with the word 'disabilities' is that it immediately suggests
an inability to see or hear or walk or do other things that many of us take for granted.
But what of people who can't feel? Or talk about their feelings? Or manage their feelings in
constructive ways? What of people who aren't able to form close and strong relationships?
And people who cannot find fulfillment in their lives, or those who have lost hope,
who live in disappointment and bitterness and find in life no joy, no love?
These, it seems to me, are the real disabilities."*

— Fred Rogers
*The World According to
Mister Rodgers: Things to Remember*

The idea that a person is unable to function "normally" gives rise to the social construction of "disability." When a person experiences changes in body functions or mental health they are open to being described as "disabled." Individuals may suffer physical disabilities, mental or emotional disabilities, developmental, sensory disabilities, and still others may suffer "somatosensory impairment" or the insensitivity to touch, heat, cold and pain. The mere perception of being different from "normal people" can cause stress and even trauma. Many people feel they cannot relate to the disabled experience, that a disabled life experiences a different physical reality than an abled-body's physical reality. But a "disabled" body offers new perspectives about social constructs, how a body is valued, and how we communicate. The fact is all of us will be disabled in some way at some point in our lives; the question is when.

How well we understand disabilities and their effects on human personality can determine success or failure.

DISABILITY DEFINITIONS

Dis-able, meaning, not able.

Disability is a cultural construct. Diagnostic categories reflect cultural values, so does what we call "disability."

Disability culture is about empowerment and identity in the context of disability. It redefines and reclaims disability in the context of the unique global community that celebrates awareness and empowerment in all its human variations.

WE ARE NOT OUR DIAGNOSIS

"The struggle for inclusion is going to be a long one as the evolution of "disability culture" is still in an infant stage in our country. A key function of "disability culture" is the celebration of the uniqueness of disability. It is my belief however that it will blossom as people with disabilities increasingly identify with each other and begin to express themselves more artistically and participate in the cultural life of society as a whole."

— Dr. Ben Ngubane
South African Political Activist

We often call people by their diagnosis: We say (erroneously) "Laura is schizophrenic," "Joan is a borderline." This is offensive.

A better way would be to say:

"Laura has been diagnosed with schizophrenia" or "Joan was diagnosed with borderline personality disorder."

While the term disability is commonly used there may be more appropriate terms of reference.

Person with a disability, not "challenged" or "the disabled."

A person with autism may be referred to as neuro-diverse, autistic, or an "autie" within the autism community.

For specific disabilities, saying "person with _____ syndrome."

Did you know?

- Chronic diseases like heart disease, high blood pressure, cancer, diabetes, arthritis, and obesity) are the leading causes of death and disability in the United States.

- Half of all adults have one or more chronic health conditions. Arthritis is the most common cause of physical disability.

- Mental health problems are a leading cause of disability. Three of the ten leading causes of disability in people between the ages of 15 and 44 are mental disorders.

- One out of every three to four youths is estimated to meet lifetime criteria for a mental illness.

Think about some of these terms that are or have been used across time and cultures: deformed, crippled, deaf and dumb. Note the ways they may still be used metaphorically in our day-to-day language. For example: "The blind leading the blind" or the school-yard bully term of calling someone "retard, fag, spaz, and, hysterical."

HOW OFTEN DO WE USE PHRASES LIKE:

"Stand on your own two feet."

"Stand up straight and look them in the eye."

"Take your own first step."

"Out of my hands."

Mobility

I have always had a well-functioning body however, I needed knee surgery due to an athletic injury. Following surgery, I was on crutches and needed to use an electric cart to shop. This was an illuminating experience about how people in carts are treated. I was stared at, looked up and down as though people were looking to find out the "problem." I was pushed, and overall was not treated well, by some people. This gave me an important insight into the everyday experience of people who are not mobile on their own feet.

To gain somatic empathy into the experience of what it means to have mobility challenges, spend a week using a cart while shopping in a grocery store. Write down your experiences and observations.

THE AMERICANS WITH DISABILITIES ACT (ADA)

President George H. W. Bush signed the Americans with Disabilities Act (ADA) into law in 1990. The act prohibits discrimination against people with disabilities and guarantees their right and access to the same opportunities as those without disabilities. The law provides support with employment help, local and state programs, services, and activities, public transit, telecommunication services, and public accommodations. The law defined disability "as an impairment that substantially limits one or more major life activities, a record of such an impairment, or being regarded as having such impairment."

Is your office accessible? ☐ Yes ☐ No

Is your home accessible? ☐ Yes ☐ No

PRINCIPLES OF UNIVERSAL DESIGN

1. **Equitable Use:** The design does not disadvantage or stigmatize any group of users.

2. **Flexibility in Use:** The design accommodates a wide range of individual preferences and abilities.

3. **Simple, Intuitive Use:** Use of the design is easy to understand, regardless of the user's experience, knowledge, language skills, or current concentration level.

4. **Perceptible Information:** The design communicates necessary information effectively to the user, regardless of ambient conditions or the user's sensory abilities.

5. **Tolerance for Error:** The design minimizes hazards and the adverse consequences of accidental or unintended actions.

6. **Low Physical Effort:** The design can be used efficiently and comfortably, and with a minimum of fatigue.

7. **Size and Space for Approach and Use:** Appropriate size and space is provided for approach, reach, manipulation, and use, regardless of the user's body size, posture, or mobility.

The Principles of Universal Design are copyrighted by the Center for Universal Design, School of Design, State University of North Carolina at Raleigh [USA].

 What do you need to do to make your office more accessible?

PEOPLE WITH DISABILITIES: SURVEY YOUR ATTITUDES

Directions: Please fill out the worksheet to survey your attitudes about people with disabilities.

How do you respond when you see a person who is:

Blind	Deaf	Paraplegic	Amputee
_____	_____	_____	_____
_____	_____	_____	_____
_____	_____	_____	_____
_____	_____	_____	_____
_____	_____	_____	_____

Have you worked with clients who are disabled? ☐ Yes ☐ No

If so, describe four types of experiences: a positive experience, a negative experience, a confusing experience, and a miscommunication.

_____

_____

_____

_____

_____

_____

_____

_____

HOW YOU COPE WITH A DISABILITY

Directions: Please fill out the worksheet.

Do you have a disability? If so name the disability or disabilities.

_____

_____

_____

_____

What are the ways you have been treated "differently" as a result of your disability?

_____

_____

_____

_____

In what ways have you suffered or do you suffer as a result of the disability?

_____

_____

_____

_____

How have you suffered at the hands of others as a result of your disability?

_____

_____

_____

_____

Is your disability visible or invisible?

_____

_____

_____

_____

_____

_____

_____

Share the ways in which your disability (does or does not) affect your physical health and mental health.

_____

_____

_____

_____

_____

_____

_____

_____

UNDERSTANDING YOUR FEELINGS ABOUT DISABILITIES

Directions: Nancy Miller and Catherine Sammons in their book: *Everybody's Different: Understanding and Changing our Reactions to Disabilities* suggest that we assess our feelings when we meet someone who we presume is disabled:

☐ Admiration	☐ Disgust	☐ Inspiration	☐ Sadness
☐ Anger	☐ Empathy	☐ Interest	☐ Shame
☐ Apprehension	☐ Fear	☐ Nervousness	☐ Shock
☐ Apathy	☐ Fixation	☐ Pity	☐ Surprise
☐ Curiosity	☐ Frustration	☐ Relief	☐ Sympathy
☐ Disappointment	☐ Guilt	☐ Resentment	☐ Tolerance
☐ Discomfort	☐ Helplessness	☐ Resistance	☐ Uncertainty

Think about the following questions:

- *What reactions above have you experienced?*

- *Are they different with different people?*

- *Where do these feelings derive from?*

- *What is your next step for growth and knowledge about "abilities"?*

VISIBLE AND INVISIBLE DISABILITIES

Directions: Please fill out the following worksheet.

Name four visible disabilities:

1. _____
2. _____
3. _____
4. _____

Name four invisible disabilities:

1. _____
2. _____
3. _____
4. _____

How do you feel about each of these? Why?

_____

_____

_____

_____

What might you do to deepen your knowledge of Deaf background?

_____

_____

_____

_____

_____

DEAF CULTURE

"I won't see you if you regard me as a patient." said the woman. "You will have to acknowledge that my hearing is different, but not inferior to yours."

"Why are we the impaired ones?" said another. "Why don't you see yourself as signing impaired?"

These were the responses that the neurologist Oliver Sacks received when inquiring about Deafness. This perspective on hearing disrupted everything Sacks had thought about *perception.* This led Sacks to push his planned pursuits aside, drive to the coast, and catch a boat to Martha's Vineyard-- a place not only rich with fancy boats, and wide pine floored homes with sunset views, but rich in history of Deaf culture.

"In the nineteenth century, and presumably earlier, one American in every 5,728 was born deaf, but on the Vineyard the figure was one in every 155," states medical anthropologist and author of *Everyone Here Spoke Sign Language*, Nora Groce. These statistics were difficult to assure though, she notes. Usually, the label deaf follows you beyond medical records, and onto birth, marriage, and death certificates, land deeds or tax accounts. But this was not the case on the Vineyard. Groce could barely find any written records concerning deafness. With such a presumably strong population of deaf individuals, why was there no indication of Deaf culture? Groce decided to conduct oral histories with the island residents. The locals grew up on the island in the beginning of the 1900s and carried the memories from their grandparents who inhabited the land in the 1800s.

Groce talked to one elderly woman who was born around 1900. The woman talked about her mother's puzzlement with a professor who visited from Boston to study the Vineyard deaf. "Why would someone travel all the way from Boston? There was nothing at all unusual about them, you know,"she told Groce. The professor she was talking about was Alexander Graham Bell (inventor of the telephone), who worked on behalf of the eugenics movement, and persuaded many deaf individuals not to marry. Bell believed that all minority languages in the United States should be eradicated. Deaf Vineyard children were sent away to the newly founded American Asylums, where they were taught to lip-read. Some teachers even tied the children's hands together to stop them from signing.

> ### Did you know?
>
> There are two definitions for the word deaf. The word deaf with a lowercase "d" refers to those that partially or fully lack the sense of hearing. When Deaf is spelled with an uppercase "D" it is referring to Deaf culture and its corresponding beliefs and norms.

> ### Did you know?
>
> Eugenics — is the belief and practice of activities that are designed to improve the genetic quality of the human population. It has most often led to abuses based on different diagnostic categories for health and mental function, cultural beliefs and fears, and racial and ethnic differences. It has been practiced for thousands of years and reached its peak with the Nazi holocaust, and also has included forced sterilization of people in prisons and among Native people, the Tuskegee syphilis experiment on African American men, and today genetic engineering and cloning. Scientists have now genetically modified the human embryo. What does this mean for eugenics in the 21st century?

During the interviews, when the Vineyard informants were asked to list all the deaf people they remembered, they usually listed only one or two people, though many of them knew many more than that. When prompted to recall other individuals who their neighbors recalled as Deaf, they often responded, "Oh yeah, come to think of it, I guess they were. I'd forgotten about that." Groce discovered that most everyone on the island knew sign language. This disability seemingly could not be studied, because it was not a disability. The social structure accommodated the difference, so there was no divide between the Deaf and the not deaf. One elder summed it up:, "I didn't think about the Deaf any more than you'd think about anybody with a different voice."

HABITUATION AND SENSITIZATION

Our brains are wired to detect differences. Two basic responses on recognizing differences are habituation and sensitization. Habituation occurs when, over time, we start to get used to a difference. The difference has not changed, but we notice it less and less. For example, your friend has an eye condition that has caused her eye to swell. When you first met her, you noticed it more and had a stronger reaction. You had some trouble knowing where to look, would accidently stare at times, and had uncomfortable feelings in response to your own behavior. But now that you have known her for years, you do not think twice when making eye contact with her. The community at Martha's Vineyard responded habitually to the deaf individuals. Many of the community members could not even remember who was Deaf and who was not.

Sensitization is the reverse of habituation. It occurs when we start deciphering differences in greater detail. Usually we have sensitized reactions regarding activities we engage in for long periods of time. For example, a bird watcher can pick up the many differences in bird songs, chirps, and tones much as a mother can decipher the different cries from her baby.

EXERCISE

MATCHING GAME

Directions: Match each person with a description of their work. Answers can be found below.

1. Gabriela Brimmer   4. Kathryn 'Kay' McGee   7. Eunice Kennedy Shriver

2. Judi Chamberlin   5. Judith Heumann   8. Lizzie Velásquez

3. Tony Coelho   6. Edward Roberts

_____**A.** Former U.S. congressman with epilepsy who authored and sponsored the Americans with Disabilities Act

_____**B.** Contracted polio as a child and became an advocate for people with disabilities. Founded Disabled in Action.

_____**C.** American founder of the Mad Pride movement who worked for the rights of people with mental illness. Author of *On Our Own: Patient-Controlled Alternatives to the Mental Health System.*

_____**D.** Has a rare congenital disease that prevents her from gaining weight. Writer and public speaker on the subjects of disabilities, self-esteem, and bullying.

_____**E.** A poet with cerebral palsy. The American-Mexican movie, *Gaby: A True Story*, was based on her life.

_____**F.** An activist whose daughter was born with down syndrome. Started the National Association for Down Syndrome.

_____**G.** Fought for his right as a quadriplegic to attend the University of California, Berkeley, which led to the creation of first Centre for Independent Living.

_____**H.** Advocate for intellectually disabled people. Founded Special Olympics International.

1.D, 2.C, 3.A, 4.E, 5.B, 6.G, 7.H, 8.D

WORKSHEET
ADAPTATION

Direction: Reflect on a task or activity you feel you do differently from most people.

How have you adapted? Have you faced discrimination for this difference?

_____

_____

_____

_____

_____

_____

Have you been defined by this trait? Do you consider this difference a disability? Why or why not? How would you feel if someone called you disabled?

_____

_____

_____

_____

_____

_____

_____

BODY IMAGE, BODY SCAN: CLINICIANS AND CLIENTS

This exercise can be completed to get in touch with how you feel in different areas of your body and also as a repeatable healing exercise. All too often we focus on our head and not our hearts or the rest of our body lower than the neck. We become out of touch, even dissociated. This scan can be adapted for use with anyone who wants to "lose their mind and come to their senses."

Directions: I read this exercise to my client. I make a recording to be used at home or suggest that she/he make a recording for personal use. When reading the exercise be sure that you allow enough time for the whole process. Doing the exercise yourself while you read it will help you with timing the process. It is better to go too slowly than too quickly. The exercise can be completed in stages depending upon the client's comfort level. Allow time following the exercise to discuss and process the experience, with a special focus on areas of body discomfort such as numbness, pain, or uncomfortable tingling. There may also be areas that the client is unable to access that may be discovered during the scan, that may include positive feelings as well. There may be areas of sensation that provoke judgment, fear, anger, and dislike that can be discussed and discovered so that subsequent scans may be encouraged without negative self-judgment or concern.

There may also be pleasurable feelings, which can be tolerated or too sensitive to be tolerated. All of these experiences may be considered. The goal of the exercise is to relax and explore the body and to use the exercise to become more grounded, accepting, and "in touch," without being judgmental. The variations of the scan also incorporate additional self-care behaviors to address areas of pain or discomfort or to induce tolerance of positive sensation. Finally, feel free to use this as a jumping-off point to create your own process tailored to a client's needs.

READ ALOUD SLOWLY, GIVING TIME FOR INHALATION AND EXHALATION

Begin by getting comfortable and close your eyes. You may be sitting or lying down (whatever feels right to you) and turn your attention to your breathing. Commence breathing through the nostrils and out through the mouth with lips pursed. As you breathe in, feel the air as it touches the nostrils and feel it as it travels through the sinuses, feeling your belly and lungs expand with the breath and then relax. Allow yourself to become comfortable with the rhythm of your breathing. There is no right or wrong way to feel, just allow yourself to experience the sensations. Now check in with yourself and see if you are comfortable, and if not, adjust your position. Wiggle your toes and your fingers and shake a bit as you settle in to your body . . . now bring your attention to your eyes and eyebrows. Feel whether there tension in your forehead ... now your brows and eyes. If so, allow this area to let go a bit and relax . . . continuing to breathe naturally . . . now bring your attention to your jaw, opening your mouth ever so slightly, allowing your jaw to relax, breathing out through the mouth, allowing the rhythm of inhalation and exhalation to continue as you deepen into relaxation.

Allow your awareness to travel down the front of your neck, feel the muscles from your chin and jaw as they attach to the neck and follow around to the back of your neck, becoming aware of how your skull sits on your neck. Let your head move ever so slightly from side to side and then front to back, feeling how lightly it sits, allowing it to lighten, lighten, and lighten. Feel free to adjust your head forward or backward a bit so it sits like a balanced ball upon your spine. Your neck muscles are strong but also relaxed . . . allow your self to be with your neck. . . .

Now inhale, and as you exhale bring your attention down your right arm, to your elbow, and down to your fingertips, allowing your awareness to envelop your palm and the back of your hand. Now inhale, bringing your attention back up your arm and over your shoulders as you breathe into the left shoulder, then exhale and follow your breath down your arm, to your elbow and to your fingertips, enveloping your left palm and your fingertips. Inhale and follow your attention up your left arm, to your elbow and up to your shoulder as you feel the circuit of your breath and your attention . . . . Resting your hands comfortably, place your hands slightly apart with palms facing each other. You may even feel sensation between the two center points of your palms . . . and as you breathe, let your breath travel between these two points, thus making a full circuit from your neck and shoulders down your arms through your palms.

Allow yourself to scan the whole front of your body, starting at your head and following down to your toes. Now that you are at your toes, take a moment to observe how you feel. Are there any areas of tension or discomfort that you feel? Observe this discomfort, allowing it to pass . . . not to linger there, but to allow it to release . . . . Continue to breathe, focusing on the awareness of your breath rising through the soles of your feet up around the ankles, up the backs of the calves, letting your breath carry you like a light breeze, ever so gently, feeling each inhalation expanding through your back, feeling the ribs expand and contract.

As you breathe, allow your shoulders to stay down, hands resting comfortably on your lap and watch you ribs expand outward, creating more space for your breath, more ease, and the rhythmic motion of the diaphragm. Your breath is moving through your back; focus on your experience in your whole torso, feeling neither front nor back but the whole circle of your breath, the hollow of the lungs within the space provided for the heart. Bring your attention to the heart, and as you breathe notice if there is any stress or tightness; if so allow the breath to encircle the heart and the space within, creating space, relaxed space, all that you require. Notice any feelings here, in this region . . . allow yourself to let the emotions rise and fall with your breath, in and out . . . coming and going . . . inhale and exhale.

Observe the feelings . . . allow your self to stay with this emotion . . . now, while focusing on this feeling, scan the rest of your body and observe any sensations that may correspond to this feeling . . . observe the connection, allowing yourself the gift of awareness . . . sit with this awareness for another moment . . . if the feeling is unpleasant, allow yourself to be; if the feeling is pleasant, allow yourself to be . . . breathing in and breathing out . . . as we prepare to end this scan, focus your attention on your breath, releasing feelings with each breath, and allow yourself a moment of stillness, breathing in and breathing out. No thoughts, no feelings . . . just relaxed awareness of your feet touching the ground. Your palms in your lap . . . your head being cradled by the neck. Bring your awareness to these three points and allow yourself to feel connected . . . within to without.

Variation 1: In this variation, focus on the area of the body you wish to affect and make toning sounds. Sound is vibration, and tension, pain, or numbness are vibration also. Matching a vibration you choose and enjoy to an area of discomfort helps to release tension and pain.

Variation 2: After doing this exercise, write down or mark the areas of the body that felt painful, numb, hot or cold, loose, free, or constricted. What words would you use?

Variation 3: Place on a table or floor nearby aromatic oil or lotion for your skin, like lavender, coconut, or vanilla, or your favorite fragrance. To begin this exercise, place one hand on an ice pack and the other on a (non-electric) heat pack, like a hydroculator (heat it first in a microwave). As you come to areas of the body where you feel pain or tension, choose to apply ice or heat and continue the scan, observing the sensations that develop from the heat/cold. You may even choose to alternate both hot and cold. What makes it feel better? Worse? As you come to an area of sensation, discomfort, or relaxation, explore feelings, open the bottle of aromatic oil or lotion, and place some on the area or just hold it to your nose. Observe in what ways it changes how you feel.

Variation 4: Adapt the body scan to do with your eyes open by standing in front of a mirror.

How was the experience different doing the scan with eyes closed in contrast to eyes open?

RESOURCES

Access many of these resources online at www.healthalt.org

Books and Publications:

Hockenberry, J. (1996). *River Out Of Eden*. New York, New York: Hachette Book Group.

Hockenberry, J. (2002). *Moving Violations: War Zones, Wheelchairs and Declarations of Independence, A Memoir of Life with a Disability*. New York, New York: Anchor Books.

Holcomb, T. (in preparation). *Introduction to American Deaf Culture*. New York: Oxford University Press

Linton, S. (2006). *My Body Politic: A Memoir*. Ann Arbor, MI: University of Michigan Press.

Mackelprang, R. W., & Salsgive, R. O. (2009). *Disability: A Diversity Model Approach in Human Service Practice* .Chicago, Illinois: Lyceum Books.

Shapiro, J. P. (1994) *No Pity: People with Disabilities Forging a New Civil Rights Movement*. New York, New York: Broadway Books.

The Principles of Universal Design are copyrighted by the Center for Universal Design, School of Design, State University of North Carolina at Raleigh [USA].

http://www.humancentereddesign.org/universal-design/principles-universal-design

Movies/Videos:

A.B.L.E. Tech: Achieving Better Life Experiences for People with Injury, Disability and Aging Challenges Through 21st Century Technologies
The panelists in the following video suggest that technology is quickly reaching a point at which the concept of disability will begin to disappear. Listen as these panelists point to the pending changes.
http://techtv.mit.edu/videos/16244-a-b-l-e-tech-achieving-better-life-experiences-for-people-with-injury-disability-and-aging-challenges.

Her Name Is Sabine. Sandrine Bonnaire. 2007. DVD

I Have Tourette's But Tourette's Doesn't Have Me. Ellen Goosenberg Kent. 2005. DVD

Loving Lampposts: Living Autistic. Todd Drezner. 2011. DVD

Ouch! Disability Talk Show http://www.bbc.co.uk/podcasts/series/ouch

This American Life
544: Batman (January 9, 2015)
http://www.thisamericanlife.org/radio-archives/episode/538/is-this-working

This American Life
538: Is This Working? (October 17, 2014)
http://www.thisamericanlife.org/radio-archives/episode/538/is-this-working

Reel Abilities: NY Disabilities Film Festival is the largest festival in the country dedicated to promoting awareness and appreciation of the lives, stories and artistic expressions of people with different disabilities.
http://www.reelabilities.org/

Web Resources:
Stereotypes of Disabilities
http://www.npr.org/programs/disability/ba_shows.dir/children.dir/highlights/stereot.html

Mobility International USA
Provides a rich resource section about disabilities:
http://www.miusa.org/resource/tipsheet/assessmentforms

United Spinal Organization

To read more on disability etiquette see the United Spinal Organization PDF: http://www.unitedspinal.org/

Epilogue

"The struggle is inner: Chicano, Indio, American Indian, Mojado, Mexicano, immigrant Latino, Anglo in power, working class Anglo, Black, Asian—our psyches resemble the border towns and are populated by the same people. The struggle has always been inner, and is played out in outer terrains. Awareness of our situation must come before inner changes, which in turn come before changes in society. Nothing happens in the "real" world unless it first happens in the images in our heads."

— Gloria Evangelina Anzaldúa, Tejana
Scholar, Poet and Activist

As clinicians we concentrate on knowing who we are in order to be effective, competent, and authentic, as we care for our clients. We undergo our own counseling or psychotherapy, explore the motives for our work and study and practice ethics so that we do no harm while optimizing what we do right.

Yet our training seldom includes learning about diversity in all its many manifestations: culture, ethnicity, sexual orientation or the (dis) abilities we may all experience. Where it does include training, it often remains theoretical or research-based and seldom provides us with the opportunity to dig deeply into our own stories as they inform our beliefs and attitudes.

This workbook fills that learning gap and encourages us to understand more deeply about who we are and where we come from. It creates new paths of insights and learning for us as clinicians and in turn to use with our clients. **This workbook is designed as a jumping off point for your own creativity and ideas; as you modify and add to these exercises so they "speak the language" of your clients.**

Return to this book again and again, as you encounter new clients, explore new learning with colleagues or if you have new questions about the changing landscape of identity and self in the wonderfully diverse social environment in which we conduct our daily practice of authentic, empathic presence with those we serve.

References

For your convenience, you may download a PDF version of the handouts in this book from our dedicated website: go.pesi.com/multicultural

Berger, S. A. (2011). *The five ways we grieve: Finding your personal path to healing after the loss of a loved one.* Boston: Trumpeter Books

Butler-Sweet, C. (2011). 'Race isn't what defines me': Exploring identity choices in transracial, biracial, and monoracial families. *Social Identities: Journal For The Study Of Race, Nation And Culture, 17*(6), 747-769

Callard, F. (2008). *Stigma: A guidebook for action: Tackling the discrimination, stigma and social exclusion experienced by people with mental health problems and those close to them.* NHS Health Scotland, King's College London Institute of Psychiatry.

Charles, C. (1986). Mental health services for Haitians. In H. P. Lefley, & P. B. Pedersen (Eds.), *Cross cultural training for mental health professionals* (pp. 183-198). Springfield, IL: Thomas Publishers.

Cheng, S. (1996). A critical review of Chinese Koro. *Culture, Medicine and Psychiatry, 20*(1), 67-82.

Coll, K. M., Freeman, B., Robertson, P., Cloud, E. I., Two Dogs, E. I. C., & Two Dogs, R. (2012). Exploring Irish multigenerational trauma and its healing: Lessons from the Oglala Lakota (Sioux). *Advances in Applied Sociology, 2*(2), 95-101.

Crozier, I. (2012). Making up Koro: Multiplicity, psychiatry, culture, and penis-shrinking anxieties. *Journal of the History of Medicine and Allied Sciences, 67*(1), 36-70.

Danner, M. (1994). *The massacre at El Mozote.* New York: Vintage Books

DiAngelo, R. (2012). *What does it mean to be white? Developing white racial literacy.* New York: Peter Lang Publishing.

Dick, L. (1995). 'Pibloktoq'(Arctic hysteria): A construction of European-Inuit relations? *Arctic Anthropology, 32*(2), 1.

Dreissen, Y, M., & Tijssen, M. J. (n.d). The startle syndromes: Physiology and treatment. *Epilepsia, 53* (Suppl. 7, Sp. Iss. Si), 3-11.

Epstein, O.B., Schwartz, J., &Wingfield Schwartz, R. (2011) *Ritual abuse and mind control: The manipulation of attachment needs.* London, U.K.:Karnac Books.

Fiorenza, E.S., "Emerging issues in feminist Biblical interpretation" in J.L. Weidman (ed.), , San Francisco: Harper & Row, 1984) p. 37.

Fontes, L. A. (2002). Child discipline and physical abuse in immigrant latino families: Reducing violence and misunderstandings. *Journal of Counseling and Development, 80,* 31-40

Geronimus, A.T., Hicken, M., Keene, D., & Bound, J. (2006). "Weathering" and age patterns of allostatic load scores among blacks and whites in the United States. *American Journal of Public Health, 96*(5),826–833.

Groce, N. E. (1985). *Everyone here spoke sign language: Hereditary deafness On Martha's Vineyard.* Cambridge, Massachusetts: Harvard University Press.

Halifax, R. J. (2009). *Being with dying: Cultivating compassion and fearlessness in the presence of death.* Boston, Massachusetts: Shambhala.

Himelstein, S. (2011). Meditation research: The state of the art in correctional settings. *International Journal of Offender Therapy and Comparative Criminology, 55*(4), 646-661.

Kirmayer, L., Guzder, J., Rousseau, C.(Eds.) 2014. Cultural consultation: Encountering the other in mental health care. New York: Springer-Verlag.

Kramer, E. J., Ton, H., & Lu, F. G. (Study and Facilitator's Guide Editors). Facilitator Guide: Saving Face: Recognizing and Managing the Stigma of Mental Illness in Asian Americans. Retrieved from:
https://ethnomed.org/clinical/mental-health/SavingFaceFacilitatorGuide.pdf/view

Miller, N. B., & Sammons, C. C. (1999). Everybody's difference: Understanding and changing our reactions to disabilities. Baltimore, Maryland: Paul H. Brookes Publishing Co.

Nadal, K. L., Issa, M., Griffin, K. E., Hamit, S., & Lyons, O. B. (2010). Religious microaggressions in the United States: Mental health implications for religious minority groups. In D. W. Sue (Ed.), *Microaggressions and marginality: Manifestation, dynamics, and impact.* (pp. 287-310). New York: Wiley & Sons.

Nasser-MacMillian, S. C., & Hakim-Larson, J. (2003). Counseling considerations among Arab Americans. *Journal of Counseling and Development, 81,* 150–159.

Peel, Jeanne M. (2004). The labyrinth: An innovative therapeutic tool for problem solving or achieving mental focus.*The Family Journal, 12 ,* 287-291.

Potochnick, S. R., & Perreira, K. M. (2010). Depression and anxiety among first-generation immigrant Latino youth: Key correlates and implications for future research. *The Journal of Nervous and Mental Disease, 198*(7), 470–477.

Severson, M., & Duclos, C., (2005) American Indian suicides in jail: Can risk screening be culturally sensitive? (U.S. Department of Justice, National Institute of Justice, 2005).

Uchendu, I.U., Chikezie, E.U. & Morakinyo, O. (2014). Brain fag syndrome among Nigerian university students in Abuja. *Journal of Psychiatry and Brain Function, 1*,1.

Waziyatawin, & Yellowbird, M. (2005). Beginning decolonization. In (Eds.) Waziyatawin, & M. Yellowbird, *For indigenous eyes only: A decolonization handbook* (pp. 1-8). Santa Fe, N.M.: School of American Research.

Williams, J. C. (2014). *What works for women at work: Four patterns working women need to know*. New York: New York University Press.

About The Author

LESLIE KORN, PHD, MPH, LMHC, has over 40 years of experience in cross cultural counseling, research, and traditional healing practices. For over 10 years, Dr. Korn was the president of a multicultural consulting firm that designed and implemented multilingual and multi-ethnic mental health and wellness programs to reduce chemical dependency in urban Boston and rural Massachusetts. She has contributed to the design of cultural revitalization programs for mental health in tribal communities in the Pacific Northwest and Canada and has provided over 40,000 hours of private practice and agency-based clinical treatment to diverse individuals, families and communities. Dr. Korn has lived and worked in the jungle of Mexico for over 30 years where she continues to direct a public health project working alongside traditional healers.

Dr. Korn has a dual doctorate in Behavioral Medicine and Traditional (indigenous) Medicine from the Union Institute and University, a Masters of Public Health from Harvard School of Public Health and a Masters in Cross-cultural Health Psychology from Lesley University. She was a clinical fellow and instructor in psychology and religion at Harvard Medical School. An approved clinical supervisor, licensed mental health counselor, Fulbright scholar and NIH-funded scientist, she is also licensed and certified in polarity therapy, therapeutic massage and nutritional therapies.

She is the author of *Rhythms of Recovery: Trauma, Nature and the Body* (Routledge, 2012) *Preventing and Treating Diabetes Naturally, The Native Way* (Daykeeper Press, 2010), *Plantas Medicinals de la Selva,* and *Nutrition Essentials for Mental Health: The Complete Guide to the Food-Mood Connection* (Norton, 2015).

Dr. Korn is core faculty in mental health counseling at Capella University, has a private practice in integrative mental health and travels nationally for PESI teaching seminars on multicultural counseling and integrative mental health.

Study Package
Course Content and Objectives

Thank you for choosing PESI, Inc. as your continuing education provider. Our goal is to provide you with current, accurate and practical information from the most experienced and knowledgeable speakers and authors.

**Please note, your state licensing board dictates whether self-study is an acceptable form of continuing education. Please refer to your state rules and regulations.

TITLE: Multicultural Counseling Workbook: Exercises, Worksheets & Games to Build Rapport with Diverse Clients

PRODUCT NUMBER: PUB084065

Before you begin your independent study, please review this package to make sure you have received the following items:

- CE Information (Contains this page and Post-Test/Evaluation page)
  For continuing education credit(s) currently available for this self-study package,
  please go to http://www.pesi.com/ECommerce/ItemDetails. aspx?ResourceCode=PUB084065
  (If applicable, not all packages offer CE):

CONTENT

Interactive, engaging and fun—this workbook is filled with valuable exercises, worksheet, games and clinical strategies to help you become more culturally competent. Use this powerful tool to explore cultural communities, religion, spirituality, gender, sexuality and disability. You'll find unique activities to help you reflect on your own attitudes, prejudices, and develop new skills for working with and building rapport with diverse clients.

- Group Discussion Questions

- Client Worksheets

- Multimedia Resources

- Strategies for Client Engagement

- Mindfulness & Meditation Activities

- Therapist Worksheets, Exercises and Case Vignettes

OBJECTIVES

1. Describe strategies and techniques for multicultural competencies in your practice.

2. Implement new DSM-5® criteria using the cultural formulation.

3. Identify your cultural influences and use your knowledge to build rapport with diverse clients.

4. Develop new skills to overcome cultural barriers such as language, religion and different belief systems.

5. Define cultural idioms of stress among different cultures.

PROCEDURES:

1. Review and study the book.

2. If seeking credit*, the following must be completed on the post-test/evaluation form -- Complete post-test/evaluation in entirety; including your email address and fax number.

-- Upon completion, mail to the address listed on the form.

-- Completed Post-Tests must be received within board requirements.

Your completed post-test/evaluation will be graded. If you receive a passing score (80% and above), you will be emailed/faxed/mailed a certificate of successful completion with earned continuing education credits. (Please write your email address on the post-test/evaluation form for fastest response) If you do not pass the post-test, you will be emailed or mailed a letter indicating areas of deficiency, and another post-test to complete. The post-test must be resubmitted and receive a passing grade before credit can be awarded. We will allow you to re-take as many times as necessary to receive a certificate, without any additional fees. All credit is awarded based on the date the post-test is received in our office.

If you have any questions, please feel free to contact our customer service department at
1.800.844.8260.
**PESI, Inc. offers continuing education programs and products under the brand names
PESI, PESI HealthCare, PESI Rehab, Meds-PDN, HealthEd and Ed4Nurses.
PESI, Inc., 3839 White Ave, Eau Claire WI, 54703

Made in the USA
Las Vegas, NV
25 January 2024

84885543R20136